# FACE THE NATION

*My Favorite Stories*
*from the First 50 Years*
*of the Award-winning News Broadcast*

———

BOB SCHIEFFER

Simon & Schuster
New York London Toronto Sydney

SIMON & SCHUSTER
Rockefeller Center
1230 Avenue of the Americas
New York, NY 10020

SIMON & SCHUSTER and colophon are registered
trademarks of Simon & Schuster, Inc.

For information about special discounts for bulk purchases,
please contact Simon & Schuster Special Sales:
1-800-456-6798 or business@simonandschuster.com

Designed by Laura Lindgren

All photographs not credited to other sources are from the CBS Archive

Manufactured in the United States of America

1   3   5   7   9   10   8   6   4   2

Library of Congress Cataloging-in-Publication Data
  Schieffer, Bob.
  Face the nation: my favorite stories from the first 50 years of the
    award-winning news broadcast / Bob Schieffer.
      p. cm.
  Includes bibliographical references.
  1. Face the nation (Television program). 2. Television broadcasting of
news—United States. I. Title.
  PN4888.T4S34   2004
  791.45'72—dc22      2004052477

ISBN 0-7432-6585-8

For Frank Stanton and William S. Paley, who built it

# CONTENTS

# Part II
### Behind the Scenes

November 7, 2004, marks 50 years since *Face the Nation*'s first broadcast.

When I was offered the job of moderating *Face the Nation* in 1991, I already had plenty to occupy my time. I covered Congress during the week, and each Saturday I flew to New York to anchor the *CBS Saturday Evening News*. But I couldn't turn down *Face the Nation*, the job I had always wanted. From the time I wrote my first story and saw my byline atop it in my junior high school newspaper, I had always wanted to be a reporter, and I got into journalism to satisfy my

*Colin Powell and John McCain often crossed paths in* Face the Nation*'s corridors during the Iraq War. (Karin Cooper–Polaris Images for CBS)*

own curiosity. I liked to see things for myself and talk to key news-makers. How could I turn down *Face the Nation*? I not only got to interview the top newsmakers, I didn't even have to go to them—they came to me. That has to be the best deal in all of journalism.

I've since "retired" from the Saturday anchor job and I no longer cover Congress's day-to-day activities, but I have never regretted the decision to join *Face the Nation*. I can't think of anything I would rather do.

Sunday mornings are a different time on television. The food fights and the shouting matches that mark the prime-time cable programs are rare occurrences on *Face the Nation*. We have learned that our viewers are more interested in content than how loud someone can speak, and that is what we try to provide—serious discussion and analysis and no sound effects. The evening news programs bring a comprehensive digest of the day's news, but time constraints limit them to just that—being a digest. On Sunday mornings, there is time for longer discussions.

*Frequent guests over the years: Senators Richard Lugar and Joe Biden, seen here in 1985.*

*John Kerry and John McCain together on the show in 1985.*

*Face the Nation* and the other Sunday programs have never attracted huge audiences by prime-time standards. It has always been who—not how many—watched our broadcast that has counted. Sunday mornings may be staid, even old-fashioned, but it is a time when those who shape opinion and make policy watch and listen to each other.

The topics that are discussed on *Face the Nation* often become the subject that official Washington chews over for the rest of the week, and the competition among the three networks to get the key guest of the week can be fierce. Over the years, there have been attempts to change the broadcast, but 50 years after that first broadcast in 1954, it remains what it was envisioned to be in the beginning: a no-nonsense live interview with someone involved in the week's most important story.

I am not a dispassionate observer. Being the moderator of *Face the Nation* is the best job I ever had. I love the broadcast, and I am proud of what it has come to represent. But as I have combed through hundreds upon hundreds of transcripts of the programs that

*One-time heavyweight champion of the world Riddick Bowe with Bob Schieffer on February 2, 1997, when Bowe decided to enlist in the Marines.*

have been broadcast over these past 50 years and watched the video-tapes of many them, I have come to have a new appreciation of the broadcast. *Face the Nation* evolved into more than a venerable television show. It has become a window on history. Many of those moments have been captured on the DVD that accompanies this book. To see and hear them live is a powerful, moving experience.

I realized that in many cases, the stories behind the stories—the sometimes funny, sometimes hair-raising adventures of the producers and correspondents who tracked down the people who were interviewed on the broadcast—were as interesting as what appeared on television.

Those are the stories I tell in this book. My hope is that the millions of loyal viewers who have made *Face the Nation* a part of their Sundays for so many years will find them as interesting as I did.

—*April 30, 2004*
*Washington, D.C.*

# Part I

—◆—

# Window on History:

## The Story of *Face the Nation*

1

---

# In the Beginning
## Stanton and Paley Invent CBS News

*It is a marvelous and frightening instrument, broadcasting, as part of this marvelous and frightening century. But ordinary men must use it as ordinary men have made this century what it is. Bad men can use it to their advantage, but in free societies, only for a time—and a shorter time, I think, than in previous eras.*

*The camera's unblinking eye sees through character faster than the printed word.*

Eric Sevareid on his retirement,
November 28, 1977

*Face the Nation* was Frank Stanton's idea. Stanton always knew what he wanted—and what CBS seemed to need. CBS News had more or less invented radio news during World War II, and Edward R. Murrow's *See It Now* programs had set the standard for television documentaries. What CBS did not have in 1954, and what Stanton felt it needed, was something to compete with NBC's *Meet the Press*, a live interview program that had the habit of generating the news that wound up as headlines in newspapers on Monday morning.

Stanton had been known as the boy wonder of broadcasting. He was an obscure, 27-year-old psychology professor at Ohio State

University when CBS founder William S. Paley discovered him in 1935. Ten years later, when Paley named him president of the network, some outside the industry would occasionally mistake him for an intern because of his youthful good looks. But that was a mistake only outsiders made. Insiders knew him as Paley's right-hand man, though a polar opposite of Paley.

Stanton was a workaholic before the term was coined. Unlike the flamboyant Paley, who traveled with the jet set of his day and spent much of the year at his homes around the world, Stanton usually worked seven days a week; he socialized with few people and never with Paley. He did not particularly like the CBS chairman. But together, it was Paley, the charming showman and salesman, and Stanton, the cold, cerebral loner, who built the broadcasting giant that became known as the Tiffany network.

It was Paley's network, but those on the inside knew it was Stanton—as much as Paley—who had made it what it was. Don Hewitt, the *60 Minutes* creator, told me about one night when he was being given one of the many awards that he received throughout his illustrious career.

"I looked down from the head table and saw Stanton in the audience," Hewitt said. "And I told the guy sitting next to me, 'Frank Stanton should be getting this award—he should get every broadcasting award because he is the patron saint of this industry. He had more to do with making it what it became than any other individual.'"

To be sure, he was the patron saint of *Face the Nation.* CBS had never been able to put together the kind of forum where key newsmakers could be interviewed on the news of the week. A year earlier, Murrow had begun *Person to Person,* a program in which he sat in a New York studio, chain-smoking cigarettes, and "interviewed" celebrities in their homes that could be seen before him on a huge screen.

*Person to Person* was a fairly remarkable technical achievement for its day. Bulky television cameras could not be easily moved, and banks of lights had to be installed in various rooms of the celebrity homes. The broadcasts had to be carefully rehearsed as the celebrities

*CBS Network chief Frank Stanton, who created* Face the Nation, *was a stickler for detail large and small. He supervised construction of Black Rock, the network's Manhattan headquarters, approved the design for the trademark eye and even set rules for what pictures employees could hang on office walls.*

walked on cue from room to room. Along the way, they introduced Murrow to various family members and pointed out interesting pieces of furniture.

During one program, the duke and duchess of Windsor played jacks on a coffee table. They tossed the ball, and Murrow chuckled, perhaps because he knew that anything beyond jacks would have been an intellectual challenge for the couple or, more likely, because he owned a piece of the show. It was a far cry from Murrow's serious journalism, but as a reward to some of his loyal longtime staffers, he arranged for them to share in the profits, a deal that allowed them to make far more than their CBS News salaries.

*Person to Person* had become a hit with viewers, but it was not what Stanton had in mind when he scheduled a lunch with Paley in early 1954 to talk about a new program to compete with *Meet the Press* on Sunday afternoons.

That it was Stanton who would see the need for that kind of program was not surprising. By 1954, Stanton had become the leading advocate for news among the CBS hierarchy. It was Paley who had built the entertainment side of CBS, Stanton who had kept the books and, more important, kept the company out of trouble with the government in what was then a carefully regulated industry. It was Stanton who had seen to it that CBS complied with government-mandated obligations to perform certain public service in return for use of the public airwaves.

When Stanton came to Paley's attention in 1935, few, including Paley, would have guessed that Stanton would be given so much responsibility. What had caught Paley's attention was young Professor Stanton's Ph.D. dissertation. It carried a daunting title, "A Critique of Present Methods and a New Plan for Studying Radio Listening Behavior." The title might have discouraged the average reader, but Paley was no ordinary reader. He understood exactly what Stanton was exploring: why people react positively to some radio programs and negatively to others. Paley had already built a successful radio network with seed money from his father's cigar factory. If Stanton could show him how to get more people to listen, that was news he could use.

Years before he hired Stanton, Paley had concluded that radio was the next great advertising medium. He had watched cigar sales at his father's factory increase from 400,000 a day to more than a million a day when his father advertised on an early radio show. If you could do that with cigars, Paley decided, then it could be done with other products. Rather than sell cigars, Paley wanted to create a place that sold advertising to the people who made the cigars and other products. Paley had begun with 12 struggling radio stations. By 1935, his network had grown to 97 stations and had introduced America to such talents as Bing Crosby and Kate Smith. His stations carried programs from as far away as the South Pole when the explorer Admiral Byrd had beamed back progress reports on his expedition to Paley's network. By then, Paley's network had more listeners than either the Red or Blue networks, which NBC owned, and it was a robust business, turning a profit that year of $2,810,079, more than either of the NBC outlets.

Paley wanted Stanton to help him understand who was listening to the radio, what they liked and what they didn't and, most impor-

*(l-r) Eric Sevareid, Douglas Edwards, Robert Trout (seated), John Daly, and editor Jesse Zousmer, part of CBS News's all-star team of correspondents in the 1950s. (George Herman Collection)*

tant, what kinds of programs would draw more people to listen. And then there was that new medium, television—radio with pictures. Paley wanted to know what its potential was. Stanton, he believed, could help him determine that.

CBS had begun experimental TV broadcasts in 1931 and by the end of the year was broadcasting seven hours of programming a day.

Nothing if not a salesman, when Paley made up his mind to go after Stanton, he pulled out all the stops. He sent a telegram to the young professor that began, "I don't know of any other organization where your background and experience would count so heavily in your favor or where your talents would find so enthusiastic a reception."

Three days later, Stanton accepted Paley's offer, drove to New York in his Model A Ford and settled in as the number three man in a three-man audience research office. His salary was $55 a week.

Stanton's responsibilities grew quickly. In ten years, he had become CBS president, and by 1954, when he began to think about creating the program that became *Face the Nation*, he had become the respected voice who spoke for an entire industry.

Within CBS, he had become the executive who supervised the news division, set its standards and looked out for it.

Some five decades later as *Face the Nation* was approaching its Golden Anniversary, I asked Stanton what caused him to create such a program.

He was 95 years old when we talked, long since retired from the company he had run for 25 years, and at times he had difficulty speaking.

But he was direct and to the point, and he needed no notes to jog his memory. Nor did he mince words.

"We were suffering on that front," he told me. "We needed a broadcast where newsmakers could be questioned in a live setting. NBC had one and we didn't. I thought we had the responsibility to provide one."

*Meet the Press*, which was broadcast on NBC, was actually owned by Lawrence Spivak, who had created it as a vehicle to promote his

*CBS founder William S. Paley was often seen with show business stars like Jack Benny, left, and Milton Berle. It was Paley who lured the big stars to CBS, while Frank Stanton ran the store.*

magazine *The American Mercury*. Sunday after Sunday, what public officials said on *Meet the Press* wound up in the next day's newspapers.

"We had tried several approaches, but we had never reached their level, and I wanted to do something about that," Stanton remembered.

For sure, some of the early efforts on CBS had been less than successful. Walter Cronkite had joined CBS in 1950 and was host for one of the earliest shows, and when Spivak learned that Cronkite planned to interview a U.S. senator, he called in a rage and threatened to sue him for "stealing our format." Cronkite argued that no one had a monopoly on interviewing U.S. senators and went ahead with the broadcast, but he was unnerved by Spivak's call.

"It was the first time anyone ever threatened to sue me personally," Cronkite told me. "I couldn't believe he had a case, but it shook me up to the point that when I signed off the broadcast, I said, 'Thanks for joining us on *Meet the Press.*' "

Stanton told me that when he met with Paley over lunch to talk about creating a program like *Meet the Press*, he was surprised to find that Paley shared his enthusiasm for such an interview broadcast. Paley differed only on approach.

"I proposed that we do it in-house, but he wanted to farm it out to an independent producer, as NBC had done in the beginning," Stanton said. "He liked those headlines that *Meet the Press* generated, but he didn't like those phone calls that he sometimes got from government officials who were upset by something that our news department had done."

(Paley once told Murrow that complaints he received about one of Murrow's broadcasts had given him a stomachache.)

"He thought letting an outside group do the broadcast gave us a safety margin," Stanton said. "If an outside group did something embarrassing, you could get rid of them, but I argued that if we did it ourselves, it would add to the credibility of the news organization we were trying to build, and in the end he agreed with me and was proud of what *Face the Nation* eventually became."

Such questions seem almost quaint today, but they were hardly unusual in those days when even those who were shaping network television were still groping with what it actually was and how it should be used.

Television plays such a dominant role in American life that even those of us who have been a part of it forget just how young the industry really is. Consider this: As the decade of the 1950s opened, just four years before the first *Face the Nation* Broadcast there were 3 million American homes with televisions. Ten years later, 45 million homes had at least one television set.

The 1950s were the formative years for television news. Programming practices and patterns that are still in use today—running similar programs such as soap operas in continuous blocks (a Stanton innovation), political coverage, evening news broadcasts, and the concept of prime time—were all developed in the 1950s. Well into the 1950s, broadcasters were still pondering basic questions about television's responsibilities as a news service: Was an industry whose stations were licensed by the government really on equal ground with newspapers? Did it have the full rights and privileges accorded by the First Amendment as the newspapers did? Or was it more akin to the movie newsreels, which featured amalgams of carefully scripted speeches and staged events such as the Easter Parade? A monthly film short called *Monkeys ARE the Craziest People* remains my personal favorite from that era.

Even by the early 1950s, the rules and standards that today's journalists take for granted while conducting interviews were still being worked out. Cronkite remembered that politicians sometimes arrived at his Washington studio demanding to know in advance what questions would be asked.

"Early in his career, Lyndon Johnson actually brought along a list of questions he wanted to be asked when he showed up for one interview," Cronkite said. "When I told him we couldn't do that, he left the set and went into the hall to leave. It was just minutes before we were going on the air, and I thought we were going to have an interview show and no one to interview but I talked him into coming back. He agreed to go on, but we didn't get much but 'yeps' and 'nos' from him that day."

By the middle of the decade, standards had evolved to the point that CBS canceled what would have been a major scoop—a scheduled interview with Soviet Foreign Minister V. M. Molotov—because the Soviet official demanded to see questions in advance.

With Paley's approval, *Face the Nation* was launched in the fall of 1954. Ted Koop, the Washington Bureau chief, was the first moderator; six men and one woman, Lesley Stahl, have followed him. Despite numerous attempts to change it over the years, *Face the Nation* has remained essentially the program that Stanton envisioned—a forum where key newsmakers are interviewed about the big story of the week.

*Ed Murrow's brilliant producer, Fred Friendly, was not infallible. He converted* Face the Nation *from an interview program to a weekly prime-time debate on national issues, and it proved a disaster.*

Keeping that format intact has not always been easy. From the first broadcast, some worried that the program would be too much "inside baseball"—Washington insiders talking to Washington insiders about topics that would be of little interest to those outside Washington. It is a concern that has continued through the years.

At one point during my tenure, a since departed CBS News executive suggested the program needed more spice and suggested relocating it in Los Angeles so it could focus on entertainment news, an idea that was wisely dropped.

In another attempt to broaden the program's appeal, a rock star named Boy George was interviewed, the first and last time, as far as we know, that a cross-dresser appeared on the broadcast.

When Ed Murrow's producer, Fred Friendly, was briefly given responsibility for the program in 1961, he dropped the interview format and converted it into a weekly debate on various current issues. CBS News correspondent Howard K. Smith was named moderator, and each week, two informed public officials were chosen to stand behind podiums and debate topics such as: Is big government good or bad?

The program was moved from Sunday afternoons to prime time. Not surprisingly, given the choice between a Friday night debate on the merits of big government and entertainment programming, ratings plummeted. The program became a financial disaster and was soon canceled. It did not air again until a Sunday morning in 1963 when it returned to its original format and Martin Agronsky was named moderator.

What each generation of producers discovered was that what viewers want from the broadcast is the serious, no-frills interview format that Stanton envisioned.

For all the attempts to change it, *Face the Nation* survived to become television's second oldest program. *Meet the Press*, the NBC program that *Face the Nation* had been created to compete against, is the oldest.

From the Red Scares of the 1950s to the collapse of communism in the 1980s and the impeachment trial of Bill Clinton in the 1990s, from Vietnam and Watergate to 9/11, key newsmakers from Joe McCarthy to Monica Lewinsky's lawyer have come to *Face the Nation* to argue their side of the story of the day.

By September 2004, 4,862 newsmakers—every man who has served as president and vice president since Eisenhower, scores of princes and potentates, senators and members of Congress—have appeared on *Face the Nation's* 2,450 broadcasts.

When Nikita Khrushchev was interviewed on *Face the Nation*, he became the first Communist leader ever to be interviewed on television. The week after Fidel Castro came to power in Cuba, he arrived for a *Face the Nation* interview in a Havana ballroom accompanied by 200 armed men—but he told his interviewers not to worry because "we are men of love."

The most frequent guest by far has been Bob Dole, the former senator and Republican presidential candidate, who has appeared 63 times. Another Republican senator, Arizona's John McCain, ranks second. Former House Budget Committee chairman and one-time Clinton White House chief of staff Leon Panetta and Delaware senator Joe Biden, once a presidential candidate and long one of Capitol Hill's key foreign policy experts, have been the most frequent Democratic Party guests.

Despite some breathtakingly close calls, *Face the Nation's* producers have always managed to get *something* on the air.

The late New York senator Daniel Patrick Moynihan once disappeared shortly before a broadcast. It turned out he had just gone outside to catch a breath of air before the program. Producers found him just minutes before the broadcast aired.

A Russian embassy official in Washington once cancelled several hours before the broadcast because of a bad cold, but when Jeanne Edmunds, a producer at the time, told him to "at least find a substitute with a Russian accent," he arranged to get a Russian journalist to show up in his place.

During the Vietnam War, producer Prentiss Childs and correspondent Marvin Kalb traveled all the way to Saigon to interview the man then serving as president of South Vietnam, only to discover on the day of their arrival that he had been deposed. A guest was found in Washington to replace him.

The only program that ever began without the featured guest was September 6, 1970, when George Meany, the aging president of the AFL-CIO, who was the only guest that Sunday, misunderstood what time the broadcast was to begin and showed up 15 minutes late.

George Herman, who was the moderator, had prepared a 30-minute broadcast on the photography of Henri Cartier-Bresson for just such emergencies, and the tape was pulled off the shelf and run. In those days, *Face the Nation* was taped a half-hour before it was broadcast in Washington, and when it came time for the program to air in Washington, Herman interviewed Meany live.

Meany never did seem to comprehend what he had done. Her-

*Ed Murrow invented radio news during World War II and in the 1950s set the standard for television documentaries.*

man was the union shop steward for the CBS News people who belonged to AFTRA, the broadcasting guild, and as he tried to make small talk before the delayed interview, he teased Meany for "letting down a fellow union man."

"Well, yours is not much of a union," Meany responded.

Such are the hazards of producing a live broadcast on Sunday morning, when offices are closed and officials and their aides are hard to reach and the possibility increases that newsmakers' alarm clocks may not go off.

We also go into every broadcast knowing that if the news changes suddenly, we'll have to rearrange our best-laid plans and start over to give our viewers as much information about the breaking news as we can. When Princess Diana died, we junked everything at 8:00 A.M. that we had planned for that day's broadcast and did an entirely different program when *Face the Nation* aired two and a half hours later.

Frankly, that's what makes the job challenging and, when we do a good job, rewarding. But it's also why Ellen Wadley, a longtime CBS producer in the 1960s and 1970s, spoke for all of us when someone asked her to describe her main responsibilities at *Face the Nation*.

"Mostly," she said, "we knock on wood."

---

# In the Age of Fear

## McCarthy, Blacklists and the Red Scare

*We must not confuse dissent with disloyalty. We must remember always that accusation is not proof, and that conviction depends upon evidence and due process of law. We will not walk in fear, one of another. We will not be driven by fear into an age of unreason if we dig deep in our history and our doctrine and remember that we are not descended from fearful men, not from men who feared to write, to speak, to associate with, and to defend causes which were for the moment unpopular.*

Edward R. Murrow, March 9, 1954

*Face the Nation*'s first broadcast came at an ugly time in America and the first guest was the man responsible for much of the ugliness, Wisconsin senator Joe McCarthy.

Ted Koop, the Washington Bureau chief who helped arrange McCarthy's appearance, didn't know quite what to expect when McCarthy arrived at the CBS studio on the Sunday afternoon of November 7, 1954. The following day, the Senate was to begin debating whether McCarthy should be punished in some way for conduct unbecoming a senator, so no one expected him to be in good humor, and he wasn't. The interview was contentious and McCarthy argumentative.

But to the relief of Koop and the other reporters, McCarthy had not come armed as he had several years earlier during an appearance on NBC's *Meet the Press*. McCarthy had been worried then, he said, about death threats, and he had kept a pistol in his lap throughout the interview. The panel interviewing him had not noticed the pistol until after the interview had begun and had said nothing.

If Koop did not know what to expect of McCarthy, he did know McCarthy was exactly the kind of guest CBS president Frank Stanton had envisioned for the new program. Stanton wanted *Face the Nation* to be the place where the key figure in the major story of the week was questioned, and McCarthy was just that. The coming Senate debate over whether McCarthy should be punished for his irresponsible behavior was the big story that week, and no figure was more key to that story than the man whose fate was about to be debated. In today's TV parlance, Joe McCarthy was a "big get."

McCarthy didn't invent "McCarthyism," as Ed Murrow's producer, Fred Friendly, used to say, but he exploited it. As the United States and the Soviet Union became locked in an ideological struggle after World War II, fear that the Soviets were trying to undermine the U.S. government were rampant. With both sides possessing nuclear weapons and with Soviet officials bragging they would someday convert the entire world to communism, some of the fears were justified. Had the United States not opposed them, they may well have succeeded. But McCarthy had seized on the fear and had tried to turn it to his own advantage, and in the process ruined the lives and careers of many innocent people.

In February 1950, McCarthy had been an obscure backbencher looking for ways to make his mark as a senator when he announced in a speech in Wheeling, West Virginia, that he held in his hand a list of 205 Communists who were working at the State Department.

He never found the Communists, and the speech was no more than a bad publicity stunt, but for more than three years, he terrorized the country with charges that agents of the Communist Party had infiltrated the government and were working to overthrow it.

The charges seem almost ridiculous today, but nothing was out of bounds for McCarthy. At one point he questioned the loyalty of President Dwight D. Eisenhower, accused conservative publications such as the *Saturday Evening Post* and *Time* magazine of carrying the official line of the Communist Party and two days after his appearance on *Face the Nation* called the bipartisan Senate committee that had investigated him "the unwitting handmaiden of the Communist Party."

Ludicrous they may have been, but the charges had turned America into a place of witch hunts and blacklists. Even CBS, the home of Edward R. Murrow, whose reports on McCarthy would eventually be a major reason for his downfall, kept a list of people who could not be hired because of their alleged ties to the Communist Party. The blacklists came from annual publications called *Aware, Red Channels* and *Counterattack.* The publications were collections of half-truths, innuendo, and outright lies compiled by self-appointed policemen who offered no proof of their accusations. Yet as Murrow producer Friendly would later report, they became the bibles for broadcast companies, sponsors, advertising agencies and motion picture studios.

In his book *Due to Circumstances Beyond Our Control,* Friendly described the publications as "catalogues of quarter truths, gossip, and confessions of informers of questionable credentials." But to be listed by them, Friendly said, "was the death warrant for the careers of hundreds of talented actors, playwrights, directors, composers, authors and editors." Fear of being accused of Communist leanings (which broadcasters feared would lead to advertising cancellations) was so pervasive, Friendly said, that the broadcast industry "responded to self-appointed policemen and blacklists as though they were part of the constitutional process."

Andy Rooney, then a young comedy writer for Arthur Godfrey, said CBS and the sponsors were more aware of Lawrence Johnson, a Syracuse supermarket operator who published *Red Channels,* than they were of McCarthy. "Every executive in broadcasting read *Red Channels,*" Rooney told me, "and people were hired and not hired because of it. They were scared stiff of Johnson."

*As his Senate colleagues prepared to debate whether he ought to be censured, Wisconsin Senator Joe McCarthy came on* Face the Nation *and accused them of holding a lynching bee. He was the broadcast's first guest.*

In December 1950, fear of McCarthy had caused CBS executives to circulate a "questionnaire" to all its employees asking whether they "were or had ever been members of the Communist Party or had been employed by organizations that were run by Communists."

Rooney said Frank Stanton and CBS chairman Bill Paley despised McCarthy but didn't exactly distinguish themselves professionally in the way they opposed him. Paley called the questionnaires a "very small step compared to what most corporations were doing by way of protecting themselves against the onslaught of McCarthy and people of that kind." But CBS employees were outraged; they saw the questionnaires as "loyalty oaths" and looked to Murrow for leadership on what to do.

To their disappointment, Murrow signed the document, saying CBS employees had "no real choice," an act that would embarrass him for the rest of his life.

One of the few CBS employees who did not sign the questionnaire was Rooney, who has always acted like, well, Andy Rooney. He returned the form saying he could not accurately report whether he had ever worked for a Communist until he knew whether Paley and Stanton were Communists. He never heard back.

That McCarthy had agreed to appear on that first *Face the Nation* broadcast is somewhat surprising in that just months earlier, it was CBS that had aired Murrow's historic *See It Now* broadcast, the program that would have so much to do with McCarthy's eventual demise.

It had been a remarkable broadcast. Murrow and Friendly had done what television does best: they had allowed McCarthy to do himself in by assembling film clips of McCarthy's attacks on congressional witnesses. After each clip, Murrow would then appear on camera and simply show the factual inaccuracy of McCarthy's statements. The country was used to McCarthy's bullying tactics, but Murrow had shown him to be someone whose smears and allegations bore no relation to the truth.

Murrow's reports were not the fatal blow for McCarthy, but they were the beginning of his downfall. In the next months, he would take on the Army in a series of televised hearings that ran for 35 days. To the chagrin of Murrow and Friendly, the hearings were carried live only on ABC, but it was during those hearings that the Army's exasperated civilian counsel, Joseph Welch, responded to one of McCarthy's bullying tactics by asking, "Senator, have you no sense of decency, sir? At long last, have you left no sense of decency?"

That remark had captured the growing resentment against McCarthy and had turned Welch into an overnight American folk hero. Embarrassed by McCarthy's tactics and smears, senators soon took steps to strip him of his committee chairmanship, and shortly after, a bipartisan committee recommended that the entire Senate censure him.

It was on the eve of that debate on censure that McCarthy

arrived for the *Face the Nation* interview. CBS and Murrow may have been among his chief tormentors, but as others would do in succeeding years, McCarthy came to the broadcast hoping to use the new program to take his case over the heads of his accusers and directly to the American people. Instead, as would sometimes happen to others with similar intentions in succeeding years, he only dug himself a deeper hole.

By today's standards and styles, the new program began in an odd way.

It aired at 2:30 P.M. on Sunday. This was in the era before professional football came to television, and Sunday afternoons were devoted to public affairs and cultural programming. So perhaps it was in keeping with the gentility of the period that Ted Koop, the moderator, simply looked into the camera and began the program by saying, "How do you do?"

Except for Koop, the CBS Washington Bureau chief, there were no CBS News correspondents on the broadcast. Instead, two newspaper reporters, William H. Lawrence of the *New York Times* and William Hines of the *Washington Star*, were in the studio with Koop and McCarthy. To make the broadcast different from *Meet the Press*, two other questioners were stationed outside the studio. Moderator Koop proudly noted that Jep Cadou, the Indiana manager of the International News Service, was standing by in Indianapolis, "nearly 800 miles away with a question of interest to the Midwest."

The other outside reporter, Frank Gibney of *Newsweek*, was in "New York, with a question of interest to the Eastern Seaboard," Koop added.

The program would soon turn contentious, but the first questions were softballs.

When Koop said, "Come in Jep Cadou," Cadou asked if the senator believed the cards were stacked against him.

No surprise. McCarthy thought they were.

Gibney tossed up another floater. Did McCarthy believe it had been eastern liberal Republicans or Democrats "who got you in hot water?"

Again, no surprise. McCarthy thought it was a combination of the two.

McCarthy had no illusions about what was about to happen. He said his enemies had the votes to censure him. He said a Democrat had told him he intended to vote for censure not because of McCarthy's tactics but because he "had labeled the Democrat Party the party of communism." McCarthy said he told the senator that he had also said there were millions of good, loyal Americans in the Democratic Party, but, he said, "Apparently that doesn't have any effect."

The Senate committee that recommended McCarthy be censured was evenly split—three Republicans and three Democrats—but McCarthy told the *Face the Nation* panel that the committee had been biased against him from the start.

Out in Indianapolis, reporter Cadou had another softball ready. Republicans had lost control of the Senate in the recent elections, and Cadou noted that they had ignored the anti-Communist crusade for a long time.

"Do you think that if they had started earlier on the anti-Communist issue, they might still have control of both houses or one house of Congress?" he wanted to know.

The outside reporters were compiling a perfect record—three softballs, three answers of no consequence.

McCarthy said yes, Republicans would have fared better if they had gotten on the anti-Communist campaign earlier. He added, "I think [Vice President] Dick Nixon in the last two weeks did a very good job of discussing that issue."

It was believed by some at the time that the real reason for McCarthy's crusade against communism was to use it as a platform to run for president against Eisenhower, his fellow Republican, and McCarthy used the interview to take a dig at Ike.

"I was rather surprised to find our good president avoiding it to a great extent," he said. "I believe he did use the word 'communism' one or two times during his speeches."

The compliment to Nixon reminded questioner Bill Hines that it had been Nixon who had appointed the committee that recommended McCarthy be censured—the committee that McCarthy had claimed just moments earlier was biased against him.

As Hines and Lawrence bored in with tougher questions, the session grew heated. At one point, McCarthy branded the coming Senate session "a lynching bee."

He repeated what he had said at the beginning: he expected Democrats to vote against him "regardless of what the evidence says" because for 20 years, he had been showing that Communists had infiltrated the Democratic Party, or "Democrat Party," as he insisted on calling it.

McCarthy's "lynching bee" quote generated headlines in most major newspapers the next day. The *Washington Post* played the story on the front page, but McCarthy's quotes did not appear until the sixth paragraph of the story. The *Post* topped its story with quotes from Colorado's Democratic senator, Edwin Johnson, and North Dakota's Republican senator, Frances Case, who predicted the Senate would censure McCarthy but take no other action against him.

Despite the headlines it created, the program got tepid reviews in the trade press and from television critics. The show business daily *Variety* called it "more an echo than an answer" to *Meet the Press*, and the *Variety* reviewer seemed more interested in how some of the reporters who asked questions had done so from remote locations. The reviewer did concede that the interview had produced some good copy for the next day's newspapers.

*Broadcasting Magazine* was also fascinated with the idea of stationing questioners outside the studio. CBS producers had come up with the idea as a way of showing that *Face the Nation* was more than just a group of Washington insiders talking to each other, an impression that still seems to bother producers, but it was little more than a gimmick and had been dropped before *Broadcasting Magazine* took note of the program four weeks later, and the reviewer was not happy about it.

"Newsmen from communities across the country have been deprived of the chance to become television stars," he said.

New York Times *reporter W. H. Lawrence was on the first broadcast's panel of inter-viewers, which included CBS moderator Ted Koop but no CBS reporters.*

Well, there was that.

The Senate, it turned out, paid more attention to what McCarthy said than the reviewers had, and the senators were furious. Several weeks later, Utah's Conservative senator, Wallace Bennett, father of current Utah senator Robert Bennett, appeared on the broadcast to say that senators were so upset by what McCarthy had said about them on *Face the Nation* that they had decided to make the censure resolution even more severe.

Even so, what McCarthy had said on *Face the Nation* paled beside the torrent of words he hurled at senators two days later. It was then that he accused the Senate committee that recommended his censure as being "the unwitting handmaiden of the Communist Party."

"The Communists have now managed to have me investigated five times," McCarthy said. "If they fail to silence me this time—and make no mistake, they will fail—I will be investigated a sixth time and a seventh but I will be around sometime and I will continue to serve the cause to which I have dedicated my life."

Over the next month, McCarthy and his Senate colleagues traded charges and countercharges. By December 2, senators had finally had enough. By a bipartisan vote of 65 to 22, they voted to condemn him for conduct unbecoming a senator. McCarthy would remain in the Senate, but for all practical purposes, his power evaporated after that and his reign of terror ended.

By 1956, the power of the blacklist was finally beginning to fade, but it was not until 1962, when a Texas humorist named John Henry Faulk won a libel suit against *Aware*, one of the agencies that peddled blacklists of suspected Communists, that the practice of blacklisting was finally stopped. Faulk had a radio show on CBS until he was suddenly fired in 1957. He blamed it on *Aware*, sued the group, and won what was then the unprecedented damage award of $3.5 million. An appellate court reduced the award to $750,000 and Faulk collected little more than a tenth of that, but the suit was a milestone.

Faulk contended that *Aware* had put him on its blacklist not because of Communist ties but because he had been elected to office in his union on an antiblacklist platform.

With Murrow's historic broadcast on McCarthy and the debut of *Face the Nation*, 1954 had been a momentous year for CBS News, but taking on McCarthy brought tragedy as well. After Murrow's March broadcast on McCarthy, Don Hollenbeck, who anchored the 11:00 P.M. news on the CBS station in New York, had announced that he endorsed the program and its conclusions about McCarthy and wished to associate himself publicly with it.

Earlier, Hollenbeck had made an enemy of Jack O'Brian, the Hearst Newspapers' television critic. Most newspapers had praised Murrow's broadcast on McCarthy, but O'Brian had called it "slanted propaganda," and when Hollenbeck praised it on the air, O'Brian declared war on him, accusing him of being a "pinko" and "leaner to the left." The attacks were relentless, and in June, Hollenbeck, a frail man in poor health, killed himself. Even then, O'Brian did not let up. He began his column the next day by saying, "The fact of Don Hollenbeck's suicide does not remove from the record the peculiar history of leftist slanting of news indulged consistently by the Columbia Broadcasting System." Calling Hollenbeck "typical" of CBS newsmen, he went on to allege that Hollenbeck hewed to a "pink line without deviation" and charged that he had kept his job only because he had been a favorite of Murrow, who, O'Brian said, had a "Svengali-like hold on the handling of network news."

As for McCarthy, he had been a heavy drinker, and as his power waned, he began to drink even more, but he kept up with television news and, incredibly, when *Face the Nation* celebrated its first anniversary on November 7, 1955, he was among those who sent congratulations. Even more incredibly, CBS issued a press release to announce McCarthy's good wishes had been received. In a press release headlined "Senator McCarthy and Walter Reuther Salute *Face the Nation*," the network noted that McCarthy had been the program's first guest and proudly quoted him as saying, "Congratulations to *Face the Nation* on its anniversary celebration. I look forward to many more years of your informative and challenging programs."

The press release writer had put McCarthy's message ahead of similar congratulations from Walter Reuther, head of one of the nation's largest unions.

A year and half later, McCarthy's heavy drinking took its toll and he died at Bethesda Naval Hospital outside Washington.

He was just 47.

3

# The Big Scoop
## But Should Americans Be Hearing This?

*Thomas Jefferson said the American people can be safely trusted to hear everything, true and false, and to form a correct judgment about them. It seems to me that you either accept Jefferson's proposition or you reject it.*

*You can't say it's all right for some people to be exposed to ideas and personalities but it is dangerous for others.*

Frank Stanton, CBS President, July 1957

*Face the Nation* has had its share of scoops over the years, but no single broadcast before or since has ever created as much comment or controversy as the June 2, 1957, interview with Soviet leader Nikita Khrushchev.

The session came after two years of intense effort by CBS and took place at the height of the Cold War.

The United States and the Soviet Union were locked in an intense propaganda battle. "We will bury you," Khrushchev had blustered at one point, but it was a battle where more than bluster was at stake. The threat of nuclear war hung over every move that the two countries and their leaders made.

The average American knew little about the closed Soviet society

29

and its secretive leaders, and the average Soviet citizen knew less about Americans. Soviet leaders made bombastic speeches from time to time and appeared atop the Kremlin to review military parades, but otherwise, no Communist leader had ever appeared on television, and no Communist official had ever given a TV interview in his own country or elsewhere. Frank Stanton was determined to change that.

CBS had come close to interviewing Soviet Foreign Minister Molotov during a United Nations conference in San Francisco in 1945, but the interview had fallen apart just hours before it was to take place when Molotov demanded to see questions in advance. From that day forward, Stanton had been determined to broadcast an interview with a ranking member of the Soviet hierarchy and told his news executives in Washington and the CBS Moscow correspondent, Daniel Schorr, to push the Soviets to cooperate.

"We wanted to do what had never been done before," Stanton told me. "We wanted to get Mr. Khrushchev or another of the Communist leaders in front of our cameras and microphones in an unrehearsed interview, so that the American people could hear, see and judge for themselves the nature of Communism and the Communist leadership."

When Khrushchev finally granted an interview to *Face the Nation*, an estimated 10 million Americans saw just that, and the write-up of the encounter that went out over the United Press wire service began dramatically.

"The Cold War moved into American living rooms Sunday," the wire service account said, "as Soviet Communist Party Boss Nikita Khrushchev turned U.S. television star to lay down a new challenge to the West."

During the one-hour session, Khrushchev had offered to withdraw Soviet troops from East Germany, Poland and Hungary if the United States would withdraw from West Germany and France. It was an offer that no one took seriously, and in truth, Khrushchev made little news that day. But he had been seen unfiltered in the living rooms of America. For the first time, Americans could judge him directly rather than through newspaper stories written by others. It is the kind of thing we take for granted today, but then, many government officials were not sure it was a good thing for Americans to be exposed to the words of a Communist leader.

Throughout the interview, Khrushchev said he wanted to improve relations with the West, but when he predicted that "your grandchildren in America will live under socialism," it touched off a flurry of criticism from American officials, some of whom turned on CBS and accused the network of doing nothing more than providing Khrushchev a forum for Communist propaganda.

Stanton knew going into the project that an interview—any interview—with a Communist would be controversial, but he had pressed his executives to pursue the project nonetheless. Stanton had a simple philosophy: he believed the more that Americans and Russians knew about each other, the better the chances were that world tension could be reduced and the better it would be for both sides. Few today would quarrel with that logic, but in those tense days of the Cold War, many Americans were wary about inviting a Soviet leader into America's homes.

The interview had come about after Ted Koop, the CBS Washington news director, and Ted Ayers, the *Face the Nation* producer, had buttonholed Soviet officials at diplomatic receptions and bombarded them with formal requests for an interview with any Soviet official the Russians cared to produce. Working the story in Moscow, Schorr routinely made the same request every three months. The Soviets showed no interest in either place until May 11, 1957. That day, out of the blue, a press officer at the Soviet embassy in Washington called Koop and asked a series of routine questions: How long would such an interview take? Where would it be conducted? Would CBS promise not to edit it? Koop answered patiently and was stunned when the press officer said, "Then Soviet Party leader Khrushchev accepts your kind invitation!" It was the first indication that Khrushchev himself would be the official to be interviewed. Koop found it hard to believe but informed Stanton and CBS News president Sig Michelson, and a five-man CBS crew equipped with a half-ton of lights and camera gear soon joined correspondent Schorr in Moscow to film the encounter. (A live broadcast was technically impossible. Once the interview was completed, the film was hand-carried back to New York, where it was developed and assembled for the broadcast.)

Arrangements almost fell apart two days before the filming, when the Soviets were informed that the panel of correspondents conducting the interview would not only include Schorr and *Face the Nation* moderator Stewart Novins but also *New York Herald Tribune* correspondent B. J. Cutler. The Soviets said CBS had told them only CBS correspondents would be involved, and they balked when Schorr said the program's format always included one non-CBS reporter and could not be changed.

*When* Face the Nation's *interview with Nikita Khrushchev was broadcast on Soviet television, CBS Moscow correspondent Daniel Schorr became a recognizable face to the Soviet people. (Daniel Schorr collection)*

*Khrushchev,* Face the Nation *moderator Stuart Novins, B. J. Cutler of the* New York Herald Tribune *and Schorr. Khrushchev refused makeup even to take the shine off his bald pate.*

"We didn't want the Soviets to get the idea they could name the questioners," Schorr recalled, "so I called Frank Stanton in New York on a phone that I assumed to be monitored and let him assure me that we would cancel the interview if the Soviets objected to the *Herald Tribune* man. The next day, the Soviets dropped their demand."

After that, the preparations proceeded without problems—or at least without problems of any significance. The Americans set up cameras in Khrushchev's Kremlin office and were somewhat surprised when Russian technicians installed Russian cameras beside the American equipment. Khrushchev's aides informed the Americans that they intended to show the entire interview on Soviet television. (Most of it was broadcast later to the Soviet people, but Soviet censors couldn't resist editing out a portion where Khrushchev had mentioned an inconsistency with the Chinese brand of communism.) Khrushchev refused to allow the CBS technicians to rearrange the furniture in his office because he said he wanted the broadcast to reflect reality. The technicians did push a conference table against Khrushchev's desk and covered it with green felt in order to have a

*The Soviets installed their own cameras beside the CBS cameras and showed the interview on Soviet television, the first time they had broadcast one of their leaders being interviewed.*

place to set the microphones. It made for an odd-looking place to conduct an interview, but it was what the Communist boss wanted.

Khrushchev also sent word that he would not wear makeup because he "was not an actor." The Americans protested and urged just a little powder to take the shine off his bald head, but the Soviet leader would have none of it. At precisely the appointed time and wearing a freshly pressed gray suit, Khrushchev walked into the office and declared himself ready to be interviewed.

But when moderator Novins read the introduction to the program, Khrushchev told his interpreter to stop the proceeding because Novins had described the office as the place where major decisions were made.

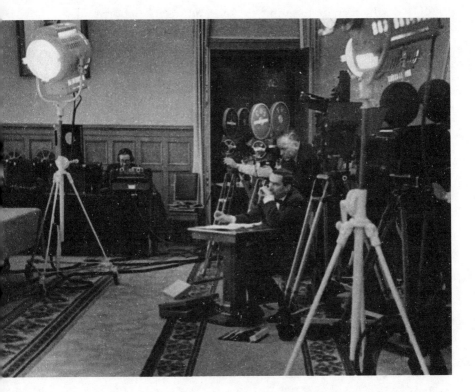

"We do not have a cult of personality here," Khrushchev said.

Novins said he was happy to rewrite the lead and started once more, only to have Khrushchev halt the interview again.

"That's when he tried to put us on the defensive," Schorr remembered. "He said he had agreed to the interview because he considered improved relations with the United States to be of primary importance and that he would call the whole thing off unless assured that all questions would serve that end. Working himself up, he pushed his chair back from the table as though ready to walk out. Then just as suddenly, he turned off the self-generated anger, an assistant director snapped a clap board before his face, and we were off for an interview of a full hour.

"He was by turn ingratiating, evasive and stern," Schorr said.

From Khrushchev's point of view, the interview had gone well. Veteran correspondent Schorr was not so sure. Looking over his notes, he was uncertain Khrushchev had made any real news.

"But I was too close to it," Schorr said. "I missed the point. What made front pages around the world was that Khrushchev had appeared in America's living rooms—real, robust and unthreatening."

Real and robust for sure, but back in America, some government officials did not share Schorr's assessment that Khrushchev had been unthreatening. To the contrary, they were concerned about Americans being exposed to such talk.

In the interview for this book, Stanton said the negative reaction did not surprise him. Even CBS founder William S. Paley had been uneasy about whether CBS ought to conduct an interview with a Communist, and some opposition had surfaced beforehand. The Catholic Veterans of America had sent Stanton a telegram urging him to cancel the project.

But those complaints had not prepared Stanton for the level of hostility the interview created in official Washington.

It was broadcast at 3:00 P.M. Sunday, *Face the Nation's* regular time slot in those days. The following Monday, it made banner headlines on the front pages of most American newspapers and got heavy play in newspapers across Europe. Many American newspapers carried favorable editorials, and most of the editorial writers congratulated CBS for its journalistic enterprise.

But there were notable exceptions. The powerful *Los Angeles Times* remarked that "those who enjoy bunk swallowed whole no doubt enjoyed the interview." The *Knoxville* (Tennessee) *Journal* called it a "waste of time" and commented, "There is a segment of the human race which is not tough minded enough to be safely exposed to any kind of Red propaganda." In an editorial headlined "Khrushchev Has a Free Shot at the American Mind," the influential *Saturday Evening Post* said, "Sometimes one wonders why it is necessary to hand the Communists quite so many propaganda triumphs just to prove we democrats are open, aboveboard and devoted to free information and untrammeled discussion thereof."

On Capitol Hill, House Republican leader Joe Martin said he had refused to listen to the hour-long interview.

"I think it poor policy to give the Communists such a great American forum. They wouldn't do it for us," he said. Another Republican congressman, Ohio's Francis P. Bolton, said, "It is high time some notice be paid to what is going out over our air waves." A business whose television stations were licensed by the government couldn't take that kind of comment lightly, Stanton told me. The leader of the House Democrats, Speaker Sam Rayburn, refused any comment on the broadcast, but Montana's Democratic senator, Mike Mansfield, a key member of the Foreign Relations Committee, scoffed at Martin's allegations.

"We have nothing to be afraid of," Mansfield said.

What seemed to anger American officials most was Khrushchev's prediction that the grandchildren of U.S. viewers would "live under socialism," but Mansfield had also brushed off that remark.

"I think Mr. Khrushchev has a lot to learn," said the taciturn Montana senator.

Not every Democrat was so sanguine. In the *Congressional Record*, Victor Anfuso, a Democratic congressman from New York, addressed a series of questions to CBS, demanding, among other things, "With whom did you clear the interview?"

"With nobody," Stanton replied.

A month later, another Democrat, Representative Ray J. Madden of Indiana, introduced a bill saying it was the "Sense of Congress" that the Federal Communications Commission require advance clearance with the secretary of state and the Central Intelligence Agency of all questions asked in such interviews. The resolution went nowhere, but the most surprising reaction came from the White House. President Eisenhower was the leading internationalist in his party and had been a great friend of CBS founder Paley since World War II when Paley had served in the War Information Office in London under Eisenhower's command. But when reporters asked Ike for his reaction to the interview, he had nothing good to say about it. Even more surprising, he seemed to take a shot at the way his old friend Paley did business.

First, he suggested the interview had been rigged, claiming it was "not the same" as one of his press conferences "where we know there are no prepared questions here and no prepared answers."

Then he suggested the interview had been arranged to improve CBS profits.

"A commercial firm in this country, trying to improve its own commercial standing, went to unusual effort to get someone that . . . really made a unique performance in front of our people and he could do that because this is a free country," he said. Garbled syntax was an Eisenhower trademark, but his message was clear: CBS had put on the interview to boost its ratings in order to sell its commercials for more money.

CBS newsman Charles Von Fremd reminded the president that the program did not include any commercials, only to have the president respond, "Well, isn't CBS a commercial firm?"

When Von Fremd followed up by asking the president if he believed CBS had been remiss in his news judgment when it put Khrushchev on the air, Ike said only, "Well, I am not willing to give an opinion on that."

Over the next week, newspapers continued to praise the interview, and comment from the public grew increasingly positive, but Secretary of State John Foster Dulles's reaction was even more acid than Ike's. He said he thought the American people "sufficiently versed in the vocabulary of Communism so that they were not fooled in any way" but noted he got his information on the broadcast secondhand.

"I didn't see it myself or hear it because I was fortunately on my island [Duck Island, his vacation retreat] where we don't go in for things of that sort," Dulles said.

Although the newspapers were lauding CBS for its journalistic enterprise, Stanton knew he had a problem with the government and within CBS itself. Some affiliate stations were concerned about the government complaints and Paley had been strangely silent.

Stanton went to work to turn the criticism around. He ordered full-page ads in the *Washington Post*, the *New York Times* and other influential newspapers and quoted the favorable reviews of the interview from the *Times* and other newspapers. The ad was headlined, "The Difference Between a Free Country and a Totalitarian Society."

Then he decided to take on the government at its home base, Washington, D.C.

He asked to address a luncheon of opinion makers at the National Press Club in Washington and began the speech on a light note. In an obvious reference to Eisenhower's characterization of the interview as the effort by a commercial enterprise out to improve its commercial position, he said, "Good Afternoon, I am Frank Stanton and I represent a commercial enterprise."

*President Eisenhower accused CBS of broadcasting the Khrushchev interview to boost ratings for profit, and his administration questioned the wisdom of allowing the American people to see an unedited interview of a Communist leader. (George Herman collection)*

The remark brought down the house, and from that moment, the audience of journalists and opinion makers was his.

During more than a quarter of a century as president of the CBS television network, Stanton would become the conscience of broadcasting and the acknowledged spokesman for the entire industry in matters of government regulation and press freedom. In the 1970s, he would risk going to jail in a dispute with the government over the rights of broadcast reporters. But he was never more eloquent in the defense of the public's right to know and the broadcasters' responsibility to inform them than he was that day in Washington.

Stanton said he believed people were smart enough to separate news from propaganda.

He recalled Thomas Jefferson's statement that the people must be "safely trusted to hear everything true and false and to form a correct judgment between them.

"It seems to me that you either accept Jefferson's proposition or you reject it," he said, "You can't say it's all right for some people to be exposed to ideas and personalities but it is dangerous for others."

Television, he told the audience, brought a whole new dimension to journalism. Now, he said, the people can see and feel what only reporters have seen and later distilled for them to read.

In a matter of weeks, criticism of the broadcast evaporated.

When Daniel Schorr cornered Khrushchev at a diplomatic reception some weeks later, the Soviet leader told him he had been pleased with the interview and the fair treatment he had received. When Schorr replied that the interview was making Khrushchev a TV star in America, Khrushchev laughed and quipped, "If American television depends on me becoming a star, it will go bankrupt in a month."

The interview also made Schorr something of a star in Moscow. The interview was later shown on Soviet television, the first time the Russian people had seen their leader interviewed, and Schorr noticed that after the broadcast, Russians began to recognize him on the streets of Moscow.

As the controversy waned, Paley issued a statement calling the

*When* Face the Nation *went to Moscow to interview Khrushchev, few Americans were familiar with Kremlin street scenes.*

interview "one of the most important broadcasts ever carried on radio and television," and by year's end, it had won numerous awards. The industry trade group, the Radio and Television News Directors Association, which had remained silent during the government attacks on the program, decided to honor Stanton and gave him its highest award for achievement.

The interview also marked a turning point for broadcast journalism.

It was considered so significant that The Fund for the Republic commissioned a study on its impact and the government reaction. The group was composed of distinguished Americans including such luminaries as pollster Elmo Roper, Civil War historian Bruce Catton, theologian Reinhold Niebuhr and Erwin Griswold, dean of the Harvard Law School and later solicitor general.

Herbert Mitgang, the Sunday editor of the *New York Times*, conducted the study and concluded the program was a milestone not because of who was interviewed or what he said or because 10 million Americans had seen it. An episode of the popular TV show *Lassie*, which had been shown later that same evening, had drawn an audience twice that size.

What made it important, Mitgang said, was that it raised a fundamental question about television in its role as news gatherer that had not yet been answered: Should television have the same freedom to report as the American newspaper? Had an American newspaper obtained an interview with a Soviet leader, Mitgang said, there would have been no questions raised about the propriety of printing it. Yet because television stations are licensed by the government, high-ranking government officials had seriously questioned whether CBS had the right to broadcast it.

He concluded that while broadcasters are licensed, if they were to reach their full potential for public service, "that should not prevent them from proceeding in the same manner as—and as part of—the free press under the First Amendment."

Stanton called it "a major step for us—for CBS and all broadcasters."

There would be other controversial broadcasts and endless arguments over what constituted "equal time" and fair use of the public airwaves by broadcasters. But from that day forward, there would be no argument that broadcasting was a news medium and that broadcasters had as much right to pursue the news as print journalists. Not until the awful weekend when John Kennedy was shot would television replace print as the medium that most Americans depended on for news. But broadcast news came of age with the Khrushchev interview. From that day on, public officials and the public would have a new idea of what television was and what it could—and should—do.

On a quiet Sunday afternoon nearly 50 years later, ninety-five-year-old Frank Stanton could still remember it all.

"I was proud of that broadcast then," he said. "And I'm still proud of it."

—◆—

# The Men of Love Put On a Really Big Show

## Castro, Ed Sullivan and *Face the Nation*

*The people of the United States, they have great admiration for you and your men because you are in the real American tradition of a George Washington.*

Ed Sullivan to Fidel Castro on his ascension to power,
January 1959

He couldn't sing or dance, and in the beginning he was just a gossip columnist who covered Broadway, but Ed Sullivan knew talent, and when CBS executives asked him to put together a variety show that could be shown on television on Sunday nights, what Sullivan came up with exceeded their wildest dreams. By 1959, the *Ed Sullivan Show* had become a television institution watched by half the people watching television on Sunday night. The formula never varied. Sullivan booked the hottest personalities—the entertainers people were talking about—and mixed them with animal acts, comedians and at least one act "for the youngsters," as Sullivan always put it. In the beginning it was called *Toast of the Town*, and it had made Sullivan the toast of America. He was awkward and spoke with a stammer, but his awkwardness seemed to make Americans love him more.

His ability to give entertainers exposure to the millions who watched his show on Sunday night had made him the most influential man in show business and one of the most influential men in America—a true American icon. But what only his closest friends knew was that Ed Sullivan wanted something else: the respect of Ed Murrow and his CBS News team. He couldn't understand why Murrow and his distinguished group ignored him. Sullivan took great pride in his newspaper background and always insisted on being introduced as the "syndicated columnist for the *New York Daily News*." The column under his byline had continued to run for years after Sullivan came to television, but when Murrow called his correspondents—Howard K. Smith, Eric Sevareid, William L. Shirer, and the others—back from their far-flung posts to talk about the state of the world during the annual year-end broadcasts in New York, Sullivan couldn't understand why he wasn't invited to join them.

Andy Rooney said, "We all knew that Sullivan had some problem with Murrow, but we really never knew what it was, and I'm not sure Murrow even knew about it."

But Sullivan's longtime producer, Marlo Lewis, said being ignored by Murrow "gnawed at Sullivan's innards."

He said Sullivan once complained, "When it involves news they won't call me. But when they hold their drunken station owner conventions and want to look impressive they call me to put on a show."

One year, Sullivan cajoled Murrow to come on his variety show, hoping that Murrow would reciprocate and invite him to join the CBS News team. Murrow agreed. Sullivan asked him several questions, and Murrow seemed to enjoy the episode, especially the backstage introductions to a bevy of chorus dancers. He described them as "easier to look at than [producer] Fred Friendly."

Even so, Murrow did not reciprocate and ask Sullivan to participate in a CBS News broadcast. Though he felt slighted, Sullivan was not one to take no for an answer. He convinced himself that the way to get Murrow's respect was to get a major scoop, and that was

Face the Nation *caught the many moods of Fidel Castro in the hours after he came to power, but almost everything Castro said proved to be untrue.*

the beginning of one of the strangest tales in the history of CBS News.

Unknowingly, Sullivan would find himself pitted against some of the CBS News people he was trying to impress—the producers of *Face the Nation*—in a race to get the first exclusive interview with Fidel Castro of all people.

As New Year's Day 1959 rolled in, it was clear that Fidel Castro was going to be a major news story. For weeks, *Face the Nation* producer Ted Ayers had been pestering his Cuban contacts to put him in touch with Castro. When Cuban dictator Fulgencio Batista fled the country on New Year's Eve as Castro and the revolutionaries closed in, the race was on among the world's reporters to get the first interview with the young revolutionary. Three days into the new year, Ayers got word that Castro would see him, and he set out for Havana. He knew the mission could be dangerous. During their first week in power, there were rumors (later confirmed) that the revolutionaries had rounded up and shot 70 members of Batista's security force. Ayers knew as well that competition for an interview with Castro would be fierce. No one was sure just who Castro was or what he represented, and every major news organization was trying to talk to him, but Ayers could not have imagined that the main competition would come from within his own company—and not even from the news department but from Ed Sullivan!

For Americans today, Castro is the aging face of communism. We tend to forget that when Batista finally realized he was about to be toppled by the revolutionaries and fled the country, he did so with the blessings and encouragement of the most rabid anti-Communists in the Eisenhower administration. For years, with the help of the American mafia, which controlled Cuban gambling and prostitution, Batista had bled his country of money and resources. To many Americans, Castro was an idealist who sought democracy for oppressed people who had been held under the thumb of a despot who ruled by murder and torture. The administration did not break diplomatic relations with Cuba when Castro and the revolutionaries took power. To the contrary, Eisenhower issued a conciliatory statement in which he expressed hope the Cuban people could, "through freedom, find peace, stability and progress."

The Cubans and the American government had expressed friendliness to each other as the revolutionaries took power, but when Ayers finally got permission to interview Castro late Thursday and flew into Havana with moderator Stuart Novins, the reception was anything but friendly. It was nearly 4:00 A.M. Friday when they finally reached the studio they would use in Havana. Ayers immediately began to make the technical arrangements necessary to transmit the program from the Havana studios back to CBS News headquarters in New York. The plan was to broadcast it over a leased telephone cable to Miami and then relay it by another cable to New York, where it would be recorded for playback on Sunday during *Face the Nation*'s regular afternoon time slot. Ayers had been told that Castro's arrival was imminent, but twice he bought time on the cable only to have Castro fail to show. What Ayers and his people did not know was that the reason Castro was late was that he was being interviewed by Sullivan at a country village outside Havana.

Finally, at 1:30 on Saturday morning, Castro arrived—heavily armed and accompanied by more than 200 rebel supporters carrying machine guns, automatic rifles, knives and small arms.

*Ed Sullivan was the most powerful man in show business, but he nurtured a secret desire to be part of the CBS News team and arranged an interview with Castro in the hope that it would impress Ed Murrow. It didn't. (SOFA Entertainment/Andrew Solt Productions)*

"I had less than two hours of sleep since Thursday," Ayers said in a telephone call back to New York. "But with the sight of Castro and his associates, I lost all inclination to doze."

And no wonder. It was some sight. Two of Castro's men stationed themselves next to each of the television cameras and kept their eyes on Ayers, the camera operators and Roberto Miranda, the director whom Ayers had hired from Cuban television.

Throughout the interview, Ayers said one of the gunmen kept a carbine leveled on him.

As Ayers described it in a CBS press release issued the next day, the interview began immediately. Castro had been wearing a .45 caliber automatic pistol and an ammunition belt and carried two .30 caliber rifles when he walked into the studio. When he took the pistol off and set down the rifles before sitting down for the interview, the crowd around him began to stir, apparently afraid he was putting his life in danger.

Ayers was clearly unnerved and asked if all the guns were necessary. Castro told him not to worry because "we are men of love."

Men of love or not, it was an uncomfortable moment.

"My immediate problem," Ayers would later recall, "was to control the crowd so the interview could be heard. I still haven't figured out a way to instruct an armed crowd to keep quiet, especially when the crowd doesn't speak English, but as soon as Castro spoke, calm prevailed, and we managed to maintain that calm for the 28 minutes of the interview."

Nevertheless, it was a tough interview, and the reporters Ayers had assembled to question Castro—William L. Ryan of the Associated Press, Jay Mallon of Time-Life, and Richard Bates of CBS News—pulled no punches.

Castro flatly denied he was a Communist—volunteered it, in fact—but said he was not afraid to let Communists run for public office in Cuba. And he made another flat statement: there would be free and fair elections in Cuba within a year and a half.

Reports were already rampant that Castro's brother, Raul, had executed dozens of Batista's underlings. When the panel of reporters asked why so many had been killed without trial, Castro responded, "Not so many, maybe two or three dozen." But he went on to suggest they had deserved to die because people in the villages knew beyond doubt that they had killed dozens of people themselves.

It was a significant scoop, but the CBS team could hardly relax to savor it. When the interview concluded, Castro strapped on his pistol and ammo belt, picked up his rifles, thanked the TV people and walked out.

"The last ones to leave," Ayers said, "were the two fellows stationed at the cameras. They glanced quickly around, lowered their guns, smiled and slipped out the door. None of us in the studio spoke until we heard loud shouting in the streets, meaning Castro had left the building."

Only then did Ayers call New York to see if the interview had been received and taped. Told that it had, he returned to his hotel and collapsed with exhaustion.

As he would later learn, Sullivan was already flying to New York with film of an interview he had conducted just a few hours before the *Face the Nation* crew met with Castro.

Ayers did get the *Face the Nation* interview on the air first, only because *Face the Nation* aired on Sunday afternoons before the Sullivan show, but the edge was taken off the exclusive when Sullivan's Castro interview popped up during his 8:00 P.M. show.

"It was Castro day on CBS," one TV critic remarked, not exactly the reaction the *Face the Nation* correspondents and producer had expected for what they had thought would be a clean, important scoop.

Sullivan sandwiched his interview between a dog act and comedian Alan King, and it was not the usual hard news interview. Nevertheless, he had worked hard to get it, and how he got it is a story worth telling. A reporter for the *Chicago Tribune*, the parent company of the *New York Daily News*, which carried Sullivan's gossip column, set up the interview for Sullivan. When word came through that Castro would see him, Sullivan hired a camera crew and chartered a plane to Havana. Not until they were aloft did he tell the crew the

49

destination. The surprise did not sit well with the cameraman or his assistants, who were not altogether sure the revolution was over.

When they arrived, they were told that Castro was not yet in Havana but would meet them in Matanzas, a town sixty miles east. A drunk wandered up, introduced himself as Castro's personal pilot and offered to fly them to Matanzas. Sullivan declined, and the group set off in six rented taxis with armed soldiers who claimed to be loyal to Castro. The scene that confronted Sullivan and his crew was even more harrowing than what the *Face the Nation* interviewers would later experience in Havana. Castro was in the midst of a speech that had already run more than three hours, and a crowd of more than 50,000 was going wild. When he finally finished and entered the 20-by-30-foot room where he was to be interviewed by Sullivan, more than a hundred of his armed supporters crowded in with him.

Sullivan began by telling Castro that Batista propaganda had "always pictured your group as not a wonderful group of revolutionary youngsters who wanted to make corrections, they said your group was 'communiste' and that you were 'communiste.' "

If Castro was a Communist, Sullivan gave him no chance to answer. He said he noticed that Castro and his "youngsters" all wore religious medals and carried Bibles and he wondered if they were all Catholics. Castro said yes and that he had been educated in Catholic schools.

Ed said he understood that Castro had been a "very fine student, a very fine athlete" and wondered if Castro had been a pitcher in baseball. Castro said yes and that he had also played basketball, track and football, which prompted this exchange:

SULLIVAN: *Undoubtedly all that exercise you did in school prepared you for this role.*
CASTRO: *It helped me very much now in this war because I find myself in good condition. The mountains, the long walking and the other things.*

Ed went on to ask Castro how he would prevent another dictator like Batista from coming to power, and Castro said that would be easy: they just wouldn't allow it. He said Batista would be the last dictator because "we are going to begin a large period of constitutional and legal government, that is our purpose."

Sullivan was clearly impressed. From the transcript:

*SULLIVAN: The people of the United States, they have great admiration for you and your men because you are in the real American tradition of a George Washington, any man that started off with a small body, fought against a great nation and won.*

*What do you feel about the United States?*

*CASTRO: My feeling for the people of the United States is sympathy. I have sympathies with the people of the United States because I think they work very hard.*

*SULLIVAN: We want you to like us and we like you. You and Cuba. Fidel, it has been a great honor to meet you and your men.*

Sullivan was so moved that he promised a substantial donation to the widows and orphans of Castro's supporters. There would later be allegations that Sullivan had agreed in advance to pay for the interview—checkbook journalism—but those close to him said he had simply been so impressed with Castro that he decided on the spur of the moment, after the interview was done, to give him $10,000.

As Sullivan returned to the Havana airport, it was crowded with many of the organized crime figures who had controlled Havana's gambling and prostitution and were trying to flee the country. Sullivan spotted one-time movie star George Raft in the crowd. Raft had played mobsters and criminals for years in the movies and was reported to have gangland ties. Sullivan made his way through the crowd to say hello but didn't offer Raft a ride, and he flew back to New York.

Sullivan's publicity agents issued a press release saying Castro had agreed to do the interview because he admired Sullivan for turning down an invitation from the ousted dictator Batista to bring his show to Havana. The press release added that Sullivan had agreed to make a substantial donation to orphans from Castro's revolution.

The episode would prove to be one of the most embarrassing of Sullivan's long career. The "scoop" had done nothing to improve his standing with Murrow and CBS News, and as his producer, Lewis, later wrote in his memoir *Prime Time*, "The acknowledgement that he hoped for from CBS Newsmen never came." Nor should he have expected it. If Sullivan thought he would ingratiate himself with CBS News journalists by taking the edge off their "exclusive," he must not have known how news organizations work.

In any case, Sullivan got even worse news in a phone call from Archbishop Francis Spellman of New York's Saint Patrick's Cathedral. Spellman told him that he had learned Castro was neither a good Catholic (Castro was eventually excommunicated) nor a good friend. Spellman thought Castro was a Communist and urged Sullivan not to give him money. Earlier that morning, Sullivan had sent Castro a check for $10,000, but at Spellman's urging, he called the bank and stopped payment before it ever arrived in Cuba.

Some months later, Sullivan was deeply hurt to learn that Castro's people had granted him the interview because they mistook him for a Communist sympathizer after he booked a traveling Russian folk dance act on his show. In his book *A Thousand Sundays*, author Jerry Bowles said Sullivan was anything but a Communist sympathizer. In fact, he said, Sullivan was a hard-line anti-Communist who had sometimes kept entertainers off his show at the merest hint they might have Communist leanings. Sullivan was not the only American who was fooled in those early months by Castro.

Relations between the United States and Cuba soon unraveled. By February 1960, a little over a year after Batista fled the country, Castro and his army had seized most of the American property in Cuba, and the Eisenhower administration broke diplomatic relations. Instead of working for elections in 18 months as he had promised on the *Face the Nation* broadcast, Castro consolidated power for himself as Batista had done before him—the thing he had assured Sullivan he would never do. The executions that the *Face the Nation* reporters had questioned Castro about continued. When the new American president, John Kennedy, took office in January 1961, he would discover that the Eisenhower administration had authorized a secret plan to overthrow Castro, a plan that infamously failed and became known as the Bay of Pigs fiasco.

By December of that year, the man who had told Sullivan, "We are good Catholics, how could we be Communists?" proclaimed that he had been a Communist "since my teens."

Sullivan made no more forays into news coverage, but in the coming years he did score a major victory of sorts over the Communists. At the request of the American government, Sullivan took his show to Russia, went head to head with the Moscow bureaucracy and won—a rare feat, then or now.

Sullivan's trip to Russia was part of a cultural exchange program, but once he was in Moscow, Russian officials blocked him at every turn according to author Bowles, who chronicled the trip. Shows were scheduled and cancelled without notice, and when Sullivan's people tried to take cameras into the streets, they were blocked.

"Finally, Sullivan had enough," Bowles wrote. "He dashed off an impassioned and nasty note to Soviet Party Boss Nikita Khrushchev."

Khrushchev, a blunt man himself, apparently liked Sullivan's direct style and promptly fired most of the people in the Ministry of Culture, which had thrown up so many of the roadblocks against Sullivan.

As Bowles described it, "It may have been the first time in history that an American touched off a Soviet purge."

It was the sort of thing even Ed Murrow would have appreciated.

Castro would be interviewed many times over the years by CBS News correspondents and other Western reporters, but never again would he be the guest on *Face the Nation* or the Sullivan show. His top lieutenant, Che Guevara did, however, appear on *Face the Nation* when he came to New York in December 1964 for a session of the United Nations General Assembly.

Prentiss Childs, who had recently taken over as producer of *Face the Nation*, remembered that "I invited him to be on the show but after I did I wondered what we had gotten ourselves into."

*Cuban revolutionary Che Guevara appeared on* Face the Nation *in 1964. Reports that someone might try to assassinate him en route to the studio "made us a little nervous," said* Face the Nation *producer Prentiss Childs, who is at Guevara's left. (Prentiss Childs Collection)*

Childs said Guevara agreed to be on the show during a tense week when someone had fired a mortar round at the United Nations building.

"It was a dud and fell into the East River and no one was hurt, but when I went to the Cuban mission that morning to pick up Guevara in a limo for the show, I was a little nervous," Childs said. "There were a lot of demonstrators around the Cuban mission, and I could just imagine someone tossing a grenade at him, so I was relieved when I got him into the car and over to the CBS studios across town."

Cuban diplomats had been telling reporters they wanted to improve relations with the United States, but if Guevara did anything that day to improve relations between his country and the United States, it does not show up in a review of the broadcast.

Guevara argued with the reporters and brushed off most questions with bluster and polemics. Like the Eisenhower administration, the Johnson administration said there could be no improvement in relations until Cuba severed its ties with the Soviet Union and allowed inspections of its military facilities. Guevara countered that Cuba was ready to improve relations "with no conditions." Asked what he meant, he said Cuba would require the United States to make no changes in its government or its foreign policy and would require no inspections of U.S. military facilities. Neither Ed Sullivan nor the reporters who had interviewed Castro during

*Guevara took exception to almost every question asked and brushed off his questioners with hard-line Communist rhetoric, but smiled when producer Childs asked him to sign the program guest book.*

those early encounters had been quite sure what to make of him. But there could no doubt among the reporters who interviewed Guevara or the viewers who watched that day about who and what Guevara was: a hard-line Communist who represented a regime that had no interest in trying to please the United States.

Certainly he was not the kind of person Ed Sullivan would ever invite to be on his show.

# Coverage a Long
# Time Coming

## The Sunday Shows and Civil Rights

*The only thing necessary for the triumph of evil is for good
men to do nothing.*

Edmund Burke
CBS network management refused to allow
Howard K. Smith to use this quote in his documentary
on the Birmingham race riots in 1961

Harry Truman desegregated the armed forces in 1948, and the U.S.
Supreme Court handed down the landmark ruling desegregating the
schools in 1954. In 1957, Congress passed a civil rights bill, and
Eisenhower sent federal troops to Little Rock, Arkansas, to enforce
school desegregation orders, the first major confrontation of the
civil rights era.

Yet it was not until the next year, September 7, 1958, that the
first African American, Roy Wilkins, the head of the NAACP,
appeared on *Face the Nation*. Two years earlier, Wilkins had been
interviewed on NBC's *Meet the Press*, the first African American to
appear on that broadcast, but when the Little Rock story broke,

both Sunday programs seemed unsure of what to do with it and were slow to cover it.

It was not as if the story had taken the programs or the nation by surprise. It had been building for months, and Arkansas Governor Orville Faubus had called the state national guard to duty a week before the broadcast and sent them to the campus of Little Rock's Central High School. The all-white school was under court order to enroll nine black students. Faubus said the guardsmen were sent there not to prevent the black students from enrolling but to maintain order. Angry mobs had shown up at the high school, and on the advice of the local school board, the black students had stayed away the first day. When they arrived the next day accompanied by two ministers, the guardsmen did stop them, and a mob of screaming white people jeered as they were turned away, scenes that were seen later that evening on television across the country. The stand-off continued, and the troops remained there through the week.

Even so, when *Face the Nation* went on the air on the Sunday after the confrontation, the broadcast stuck with the guest who had been booked earlier, Adlai Stevenson, the two-time presidential campaign loser. He had been invited on to talk about his recent trip to Africa.

On *Meet the Press*, the guest was U.N. Ambassador Henry Cabot Lodge, who was questioned about Soviet tanks that had rolled into Hungary to crush an uprising there. There is an unwritten rule in journalism that when two stories of equal importance occur, "you lead your coverage with the story closest to city hall." It's the story that happens closest to us that usually has the most impact on us, so that's the story readers and viewers are likely to be most interested in. But that Sunday, *Meet the Press* and *Face the Nation* brought in guests to talk about the far-away stories, not the story close to home. In any case, few Americans—at least few white Americans—complained. When violent civil rights protests occurred in a town or city, the protests became the local news that many white people in the local area never wanted covered. From the start, CBS News cov-

*In 1958, Roy Wilkins, head of the National Association for the Advancement of Colored People, became the first African American to appear on* Face the Nation.

erage of the demonstrations brought intense criticism from its local affiliates across the South.

Washington Bureau chief Howard K. Smith had been in Birmingham working on a documentary and had seen Birmingham's sheriff, Bull Connor, and his police refuse to stop a white mob from beating civil rights protestors. Smith was a southerner himself, but he was repulsed by the brutality. In the closing comments he wrote for the documentary, he quoted British Conservative Edmund Burke's well-known admonition, "The only thing necessary for the triumph of evil is for good men to do nothing." CBS executives were so afraid of the reaction from southern affiliates that they branded the quote "pure editorializing" and ordered it removed, a decision that would eventually lead to Smith's departure from CBS.

To their credit, journalists who appeared on *Face the Nation* on the weekend of the Little Rock trouble did ask Stevenson, "as a former governor," what he would have done about it had he been president. Stevenson archly noted that it wasn't a pertinent question since Americans probably didn't care what he would have done. After all, he said, they had twice—by landslide numbers—rejected his efforts to become their president. But he went on to repeat what he had said during the presidential campaign: that the law of the land had to be obeyed. As Eisenhower had also said some months earlier, Stevenson reiterated that he would not use force to ensure that court orders were obeyed. Rather, he suggested, such things had to be worked out by the courts. (Within weeks, Eisenhower would use force. He nationalized the Arkansas National Guard and sent in federal troops from the 101st Airborne to enforce the court order, but he remained ambivalent about integration and never took a public stand one way or the other.)

Although no African American appeared on the broadcast that year, three weeks after the initial confrontation, *Face the Nation* producers invited Harry Ashmore, the editor of the *Arkansas Gazette*, the state's leading newspaper, to be interviewed. Ashmore would later win the Pulitzer Prize for his editorials urging peaceful integration, but the *Face the Nation* panel did not appear all that impressed. By then, Eisenhower had federalized the national guard and sent in federal troops to back them up, but *Newsweek* correspondent John Madigan, one of the questioners that day, seemed more interested in whether Ashmore was biased in favor of integration than in what was happening at the high school.

"Were you interested in trying to have integration become a fact or just trying to work as a newspaperman to find a story?" he asked at one point.

Later he asked, "How much has integration been set back by all this trouble?"

When Wilkins appeared on the broadcast a year later, the controversy was still being argued in the courts, and Faubus was working on a plan (which was later enacted) to close the schools rather than let African Americans attend them, but reporter Madigan again seemed worried that events were moving too quickly.

His first question to Wilkins was, "In view of recent events, do you think it is possible that the NAACP has perhaps pursued its course a little too vigorously, with the result that there could be a backlash which would actually deter and slow orderly integration in schools?"

"No, Mr. Madigan," Wilkins said. "We do not believe that."

For five more questions and throughout the broadcast, Madigan continued to press Wilkins on why slowing down the process would not be better for all concerned.

Throughout his presidency, Eisenhower had been noncommittal on civil rights, and midway through the broadcast Wilkins expressed disappointment in Eisenhower's attitude. That prompted Madigan to say that Eisenhower's friends said the president was just trying to be "president of all the people" and then asked Wilkins if Eisenhower "should desert that position."

Again Wilkins said no, that was not what he thought.

Such questions seem harsh by today's standards, but they reflected the attitudes of many white Americans of that day and not just of southern whites.

It would be well into the Vietnam War before pictures of black Americans would appear on the front pages of southern newspapers in anything other than crime stories. In the days when Joe Louis reined as heavy-weight boxing champion, wire services always ran two photos of his fights if his opponent was white. One photo showed Louis knocking out his opponent as he almost always did. The other photo showed the white man hitting Louis, an option for the papers that did not wish to show a black man hitting a white.

Jackie Robinson, who had broken the color barrier in baseball and was arguably the African American most admired by the white people of his day, worked closely with the NAACP, but even he got fairly hostile questions when he appeared on *Meet the Press* in the spring of 1957.

Moderator Lawrence Spivak asked him, "How do you answer

people who insist that the NAACP is moving very, very fast to get the rights for the Negro but seems to be doing not enough to impress upon the Negro his own responsibility as he gets those rights?"

Robinson responded with quiet dignity, and his answer was a classic. He said people had been telling him all his life to be patient. "I was told that as a kid. I keep hearing that today," he said. Let's be patient. Let's take our time. Things will come. It seems to me, the Civil War has been over about 93 years. If that isn't patient, I don't know what is."

NAACP legal counsel Thurgood Marshall would have much the same reply when President Eisenhower had yet again urged patience in 1958. "I'm the original gradualist," Marshall said. " I just think 90 years is gradual enough.

*Dr. Martin Luther King, Jr. in 1964, when he made the first of four appearances on the broadcast.*

In time, both *Face the Nation* and *Meet the Press* would recognize the significance of the story and give it more coverage.

As it turned violent in the early 1960s, it would be television's evening news programs that brought the strife into the nation's living rooms, and by the mid-1960s, the nation's black leaders had become regular guests on the Sunday interview shows.

During the fall of 1960, CBS finally handed over all of Sunday afternoons to professional sports, and *Face the Nation* was shifted to prime time and to the debate format designed by Fred Friendly. Normally, producers of any television program want to be seen by the large audiences that watch nighttime television, but the people connected with *Face the Nation* were worried that an interview show could not compete with entertainment shows. Their fears soon proved well founded. *Face the Nation* did not draw an audience large enough to justify a prime-time slot. *Face the Nation* and Ed Murrow's prestigious *See It Now* were reportedly costing the network a quarter of a million dollars in lost revenue annually, and the broadcasts were taken off the schedule. *Face the Nation* went into hiatus in the spring of 1961 and did not reappear until mid-September 1963. Once back in its Sunday time slot, it began to attract prestige sponsors. With its small staff and low production costs, the show would become one of the most profitable broadcasts on television and remains so today.

For the most part, the civil rights struggle was the one major story where the Sunday interview programs were sideline rather than center-stage players. They provided some context for the story and were a place for those on both sides to explain their views, but the network evening news broadcasts were where Americans got most of their news about the struggle for equality. It was on those broadcasts that people saw the horror of the police dogs attacking the Birmingham protesters, the campus violence that broke out when James Meredith enrolled at Ole Miss and the huge marches on Washington.

*Face the Nation* was off the air during a crucial 28-month period of that era. For a period of months, an interview program anchored by David Schoenbrun, the longtime foreign correspondent who became the Washington Bureau chief, aired on Sunday morning, but it was soon cancelled. When *Face the Nation* returned to its Sunday time slot in 1963, it began to cover the civil rights story with some regularity, and the men whose names would become synonymous with the movement—King, Wilkins, James Farmer, Ralph Abernathy, Whitney Young, and later Jesse Jackson—would be frequent guests.

Beginning in 1964, King appeared once each year on *Face the Nation* in the four years leading up to his death in 1968. But even that late into the movement, interviewers often seemed more concerned about white backlash and Communist infiltration of the civil rights movement than they did about black progress.

When King made his first appearance on *Face the Nation* in May 1964, the civil rights bill that would finally pass later that fall was still being debated in Congress. The bill would eventually be called the most significant piece of civil rights legislation since Lincoln emancipated the slaves, and it was massive in its scope. It outlawed discrimination in public places, created the Equal Employment Opportunity Commission, barred federal funds for segregated schools and prohibited companies that practiced segregation from receiving federal contracts.

Yet the questioners that Sunday seemed more interested in whether King thought there would be new protests and demonstrations, and they asked more questions about alleged infiltration of Communists in the civil rights movement than they did about the pending legislation.

The interviewers' seeming lack of interest in the legislation was somewhat odd in that CBS News president Fred Friendly, on orders from network president Frank Stanton, had ordered extraordinary coverage of the Senate debate on the legislation. From March, when the debate began, until July, when the legislation was signed into law by President Johnson, Friendly ordered every CBS News broadcast to include at least one item about it. The *CBS Morning News* aired at midmorning in those days, and Roger Mudd, who covered Congress for CBS, made his first report of the day on where the legislation stood on that broadcast. He followed with a report during the network's noon newscast, gave a short progress report during a 3:30 P.M. newsbreak, delivered a two and a half minute report on Walter Cronkite's *Evening News* broadcast and prepared a shorter piece that was fed to local stations for use on their 11:00 P.M. newscasts.

"It is difficult for Americans today to understand just how strong feelings ran on this," Mudd told me. "In the beginning, I had a hard time getting the southern senators to cooperate. They were convinced that an eastern network wouldn't treat them fairly. I finally won their confidence, but I had to be very careful. Any time I interviewed Hubert Humphrey or one of the people pushing for the bill, I had to make sure I put on one of the southerners—Richard Russell or Strom Thurmond—who were against it. It really divided people at every level.

"They didn't allow TV in the Senate in those days, so I worked with Howard Brodie, who had been a famous combat artist from World War II. Howard was such a West Coast liberal that I used to kid him that it was organically impossible for him to draw a good likeness of Strom Thurmond—he never got one.

"Feelings ran so strong that it was the only time in all the years that I covered the Capitol that I actually saw a senator actually run from his constituents.

"Harrison Williams, a senator from New Jersey, had been favorable to the bill, but one time a group of his constituents came to Washington and when he saw them, he broke into a run. They gave chase across the Capitol lawn and he finally escaped into Mike Mansfield's office. It was some sight."

By the time King returned to *Face the Nation* the following year, Congress had passed equally significant legislation that cleared the way for blacks to vote across the South. In Mississippi, where the population was 42 percent black, only 2 percent of the blacks had been able to vote. Even so, of 20 questions asked that Sunday on *Face the Nation*, 10 had to do with whether it was appropriate for King to oppose the increasingly unpopular war in Vietnam. Interviewers had once expressed worry that the civil rights movement was moving too fast for its own good. Now King was being peppered with questions about whether his opposition to the war would slow and weaken the movement and give comfort to the Vietnamese Communists.

From the beginning, critics had tried to link King's organization to "Communist agitators," and the hunt for Communist connections was the excuse FBI chief J. Edgar Hoover used to bug King's hotel rooms. He found no Communists, but he did circulate tape recordings of King's amorous activities to people throughout the government, and King's enemies used the tapes in an attempt to blackmail King and force him from public life.

When King returned to *Face the Nation* in 1966, the reporters again spent most of the time asking about his opposition to the war and the possibility of violent protests. When he made his final appearance in 1967, moderator Martin Agronsky began the program in this way: "Dr. King, yesterday you led a demonstration here which visibly featured the carrying of Vietcong flags, a mass burning of draft cards and one American flag was burned. It was a demonstration of massive opposition to the war in Vietnam. How far should this go? Should American Negroes refuse to serve in the United States armed forces?"

King responded that he did not condone such things and was not advocating civil disobedience. He conceded that he did urge young men who opposed the war to consider registering as conscientious objectors, which, he pointed out, was neither illegal nor evasive.

At one point, *New York Post* reporter Ted Post asked, "Well, since you prize free speech, Dr. King, you realize if you had a counterpart in either Hanoi and Peking, and they opposed their country's involvement in Vietnam, as you have opposed ours, that they would be liquidated immediately and would not appear on national television the next day.

"Don't you think that in reality, in attacking your country's foreign policy that you might be defending a system which would not grant you the right that you are enjoying right now?"

King's response is worth noting.

"I don't agree with that at all," he said. "I think we can attack an unjust war without at the same time embracing the philosophy of those that we are fighting against. From a philosophical point of view, I am absolutely opposed to communism. I think it is based on a metaphysical materialism, at points an ethical relativism, a crippling totalitarianism in many instances and a denial of human freedom that I would not prefer. I do think, however, that people have a right to choose their own systems, the kind of government they want, and I think in America, we are in a tragic position of having a paranoid fear of communism, an almost sick, morbid anticommunism, which can be as destructive as anything."

Agronsky responded that King seemed to be accusing the president of having a "phobia of communism."

Despite often antagonistic questioners, King's appearances on *Face the Nation* were marked by restraint, a stark contrast to the words of Stokely Carmichael, who coined the phrase *black power*. He appeared on the broadcast on June 19, 1966, three days after he had told a crowd in Greenwood, Mississippi, that "every courthouse in Mississippi should be burned down tomorrow so we can get rid of the dirt."

Asked about it on *Face the Nation*, Carmichael wouldn't say flatly that he advocated burning down the structures, but he said they were all filled with dirt and filth. Burning them down, he said, was just an analogy for getting rid of the people inside.

But time and again, he refused to rule out the use of violence. It had been Carmichael who had said that "violence is as American as cherry pie," and that day on *Face the Nation* he said only those who were involved in a revolution could judge what means were appropriate to accomplish their goals. Martin Luther King, Jr., had raised the consciousness of white America to the injustices that had been dealt to its black citizens, but that day on *Face the Nation*, Americans were reminded that not every leader who was trying to correct those wrongs was Martin Luther King, Jr.

• • •

Despite the intense criticism from those who believed that network news coverage had caused much of the violence, from the beginning *Face the Nation* and the other Sunday interview shows gave considerable time and attention to those who opposed the movement.

South Carolina Senator Strom Thurmond, Mississippi Senator James Eastland, Georgia's Richard Russell, and various opponents of the civil rights legislation of that era were frequent guests. None appeared more often than the man who came to symbolize southern opposition, Alabama Governor George Wallace.

Wallace railed against the northern media and television for distorting the civil rights story, but he used television to argue his case. Without it, he probably would not have become a national figure who could command enough attention to be a serious factor in presidential campaigns over more than a decade.

When Wallace appeared on *Face the Nation*, it guaranteed headlines, but no appearance ever got more attention than March 14, 1965, when moderator Paul Niven, CBS News correspondent Nelson Benton, and Al Kuetter of United Press International went to the state capitol in Montgomery, Alabama, to interview Wallace after he had met privately at the White House with President Johnson. Johnson had invited Wallace to Washington after violence had broken out in Selma, Alabama, where civil rights marchers had been beaten. Johnson had urged Wallace to permit lawful demonstrations, endorse voting rights for everyone and set up a biracial committee in Alabama to explore ways to accomplish peaceful integration. Neither man spoke after the meeting, but Johnson personally told reporters that Wallace would be on *Face the Nation* that weekend and urged them to listen and watch for Wallace's response.

Prentiss Childs, who had become the program's executive producer, was ecstatic. "It wasn't often that we had the president of the United States giving our program a plug from the White House," he told me. "So we pulled out all the stops and went to Montgomery to interview Wallace."

*In 1965, Alabama Governor George Wallace tried to deflect questions about the brutal treatment of civil rights protestors in Alabama by waving newspaper accounts of protests in northern states.*

Childs could already envision the headlines that the interview was certain to produce in the Monday morning newspapers. Unfortunately, Wallace had headline plans of his own.

In the opening question, Niven asked Wallace if he intended to follow the president's recommendations. Wallace never answered that or any other question of significance that day, but he responded to that first question with a tirade suggesting what was happening in Alabama was "a national problem."

Wallace then turned on the United Press International reporter and said one reason for the violence in Alabama was that a UPI reporter there had misrepresented what had actually been happening.

Wallace refused to give in as the reporters tried to ask questions. A stack of newspapers had been placed on his desk, and he began to wave them at the reporters. He pointed to pictures of police in northern cities who were arresting demonstrators there.

"I challenge this network, the NBC network, and ABC network

to run two hours of documentary film on the controlling, restraining and stopping of the demonstrations and riots in Philadelphia, in Rochester, in New York, in Chicago, in Cleveland and in Selma on the same program . . . let the American people look for themselves and see where more force was used, who used less restraint."

Turning to a picture in a Philadelphia newspaper, he said, "Look at the clubs there and look at people on the ground being beaten, Can you see that? I hope you will just look at that."

Wallace went on that way for much of the program. As reporters tried to ask questions, Wallace either ignored them or responded with bombast that had little or nothing to do with what he had been asked.

Childs told me he was not sure Niven or anyone else could have stopped Wallace, but CBS executives felt Wallace had wrested control of the broadcast from Niven.

Before coming to *Face the Nation*, Niven had distinguished himself as a foreign correspondent who was held in high regard by CBS and throughout the journalistic community, but CBS executives were embarrassed by Wallace's antics, and Childs said Niven became the fall guy. The executives' displeasure was one reason Niven eventually left the network and finished out his career in public television.

What struck me as I reread the transcript of the broadcast almost 40 years later was how much it resembled the rants we hear so often today on talk radio and the shouting matches we watch on cable television. I wondered what the reaction would have been today. Would Niven have been criticized or congratulated? Would such a tirade be considered unusual by today's standards or just "good television"?

## CIVIL RIGHTS TIME LINE

1948
Truman outlaws discrimination in the armed forces.

1954
U.S. Supreme Court declares school segregation is unconstitutional in the landmark *Brown v. Board of Education* ruling.

1955
Rosa Parks refuses to give up her seat on a Montgomery, Alabama, bus. Martin Luther King, Jr., and other ministers organize the first bus boycott.

1957
King founds the Southern Christian Leadership Conference, becomes its leader and says he will use only nonviolent tactics to fight segregation.
The first serious confrontation over desegregation as Eisenhower sends federal troops to Little Rock, Arkansas, to enforce the court order to integrate Central High School. The First Civil Right Act passed by Congress establishes a civil rights division at the Justice Department but is largely symbolic.

1960
First student sit-ins at lunch counters. Elijah Muhammad calls for a separate state for blacks.

1961
Birmingham police use police dogs to attack protesters in an effort to stop sit-ins at lunch counters.

1962
Students use King's nonviolent tactics on Freedom Rides across the South.
Riots break out on campus as James Meredith enrolls at the University of Mississippi. Civil rights leader Medgar Evers is assassinated. In August, a quarter of a million civil rights activists march on Washington, D.C., in support of civil rights legislation. FBI chief

J. Edgar Hoover begins a smear campaign against the march organizer, Bayard Rustin, and tries to spread a rumor he is having a homosexual relationship with King.

1963

In November, President Kennedy is assassinated in Dallas as the debate on the civil rights bill continues. Lyndon Johnson is sworn in as president and vows to get legislation passed in memory of Kennedy.

Four black children are killed in a bombing in a Birmingham, Alabama, church.

1964

Race riots break out in northern cities: Harlem, Chicago, Rochester and Philadelphia. Johnson pushes through the Civil Rights Act, the most significant civil rights legislation since emancipation of the slaves. Martin Luther King, Jr. is awarded the Nobel Peace Prize.

1965

In March, police attack Selma, Alabama, demonstrators marching in support of pending Voting Rights Act.

Johnson uses the brutality of these attacks to rally support and passage of the voting rights legislation.

1966

Emergence of Stokely Carmichael and the black power movement.

Worried about King's opposition to the war in Vietnam, FBI chief Hoover bugs King's hotel rooms and leaks details of King's sexual activities. King receives an anonymous blackmail letter, apparently from the FBI, urging him to leave public life.

1967

Thurgood Marshall becomes the first African American appointed to the U.S. Supreme Court.

1968

Martin Luther King, Jr. is assassinated. Riots break out in Washington, D.C., and other cities across America.

6

———

# Vietnam

## The Ongoing Search for Good News

*We are winning. Everyone except the Americans knows this.*

Oklahoma Senator Mike Monroney on *Face the Nation*
after a trip to Vietnam in December 1964

In the early fall of 1963, Secretary of Defense Robert McNamara returned from Vietnam with good news: the war that the United States was helping the South Vietnamese government to wage against Communist insurgents was going well. So much progress was being made, McNamara reported, that he believed the American forces in Vietnam could be brought home by the end of 1965.

Several weeks later, on October 13, a slight man named Tran Van Chuong came to the CBS studios in Washington to be interviewed on *Face the Nation*. He had recently resigned as South Vietnam's ambassador to the United States to protest his government's harsh repression of the Buddhist dissidents in his country.

The interview attracted little notice, but it is remarkable in retrospect because Tran's analysis of what was happening in Vietnam was so on the mark and so wildly different from McNamara's analysis, which had been so wrong.

Over the next decade, a parade of American officials would come back from Vietnam to say what McNamara had said that fall: victory was just over the horizon. Tran saw just the opposite—disaster—a prediction that would prove correct but one that many Americans were not prepared to accept. One of the doubters the day that Tran appeared on *Face the Nation* was Marguerite Higgins of the *New York Herald Tribune*, a panelist on the broadcast. She was so dubious that she asked him at one point why he was more qualified to know what was going on there than the U.S. secretary of defense. It was an odd question to ask a Vietnamese native who had served for many years in his country's diplomatic corps, yet it reflected the attitude of many Americans of that day.

Americans were just beginning to pay attention to Vietnam. Within months, the war would begin to touch every part of American life. For nearly 11 years, whether it was a government domestic program whose budgets would be squeezed to pay for the war or a nuclear arms negotiation made more difficult because of the tension Vietnam had created with the Soviet Union, no initative could be launched, no policy undertaken, without first asking, "How will this affect the war in Vietnam?"

As opposition to the war grew, it threatened to tear the country and its institutions apart. America was the richest and most powerful country the world had ever known, yet its foreign and domestic policies came to hinge on events in a tiny, faraway place that most Americans knew little about. By the mid-1960s, Americans didn't quite fathom why it had come to that, but they could not help but acknowledge that it had.

Reading the transcripts of the *Face the Nation* broadcasts of that era is a sobering experience. In the early years of the war, the transcripts show that U.S. officials who appeared on the broadcast had little or no understanding of what was happening in Vietnam. As they did begin to understand, they often misrepresented what they knew to be the truth, or they simply lied. When Tran Van Chuong appeared on *Face the Nation* in the fall of 1963, the Kennedy administration had already dispatched 16,000 American military advisers and trainers to South Vietnam. They had been sent there

*In March 1965, Secretary of State Dean Rusk said American troops were not being sent to Vietnam to fight the ground war—but by the end of the year, thousands of American troops were doing just that.*

with little opposition. Conventional wisdom among the foreign policy establishment of the day was that somewhere, someplace, Americans would have to draw a line and tell the Communists not to cross it. They had begun to draw that line in Vietnam, and as the American government told the story, the effort was showing positive results. Secretary of Defense McNamara's 1963 prediction that the South Vietnamese would be strong enough to hold the line without American help by the end of 1965 was just the latest in a series of optimistic assessments. Certainly that was one reason that panelist Higgins seemed so taken aback when Marvin Kalb, who was moderating the broadcast that day, asked Tran about McNamara's assessment, and the Vietnamese flatly disagreed with it.

"There is no possibility at all of victory against the Communists under the present regime," Tran said.

That was what provoked reporter Higgins to ask Tran why he thought he knew more about the situation than the American secretary of defense. From the transcript:

HIGGINS: *What is the basis for your information now saying that McNamara and others don't know what they're talking about when they say the war isn't being won?*

Tran responded that he had not meant that U.S. officials did not know what they were talking about. His point, he said, was that the real war was not a military battle but a political one, a war to win hearts and minds.

"There is not a possibility of winning that war with a government which is pushing people into the arms of the Communists," he said.

Tran had resigned his ambassadorship to protest the brutal tactics the Diem regime had used to put down a Buddhist uprising, but Higgins would not let go. She noted that Tran had not been back to Vietnam in more than a year and questioned whether he had the credentials to speak about conditions in his own country. She did seem confident about her own credentials. From the transcript:

HIGGINS: *Mr. Ambassador, granted I am not Vietnamese. In my last visit to Vietnam I did go to 42 hamlets in the countryside and I found from the little people with whom I talked at great length for many days saying that they were getting more rice more fertilizer and more medicine than ever before.*

*Now do you believe that in the last eighteen months, precisely the period when you have not been in Vietnam, things have gotten better materially? I would ask . . . do you think the strategic hamlet program has any merit? Do you think there is any betterment in the life of the average person?*

Tran responded that the Vietnamese were more interested in justice than in welfare. People in America have justice, he told Higgins, so they can put the emphasis on welfare. In his country, he said they did not have that luxury, so the emphasis was on the reverse. The Buddhist protests, he said, were against the injustice and oppression of the Diem regime and had nothing to do with the objectives of the Communists.

Tran knew of the brutality of the Diem brothers firsthand. His daughter, the infamous Madame Nhu, was married to one of them and had already become known to Americans as the Dragon Lady because she bore a striking resemblance to a character of that name in a popular comic strip. It was Madame Nhu who was the driving force in the crackdown and persecution of the Buddhists. The Buddhists claimed to be protesting for more humane treatment, but Madame Nhu believed them to be agents of the Communist rebels. When several Buddhists monks poured gasoline over their bodies and set themselves afire to protest the government repression, Madame Nhu said she would "clap hands at seeing another monk barbecue show."

It was to support the Diems in their fight against the Communists that the Kennedy administration sent American military advisers and trainers and millions of dollars of military aid to Vietnam. In public, the American government had continued to express support for the Diems, but privately the administration was already disenchanted with the brothers. On November 1, two weeks after Tran's *Face the Nation* interview, the Diems were assassinated in a CIA-backed palace coup. By the end of the month, the American president, John Kennedy, would also be cut down by an assassin's bullet and the new president, Lyndon Johnson, would inherit the war.

We would later learn from the Pentagon Papers and other secret documents that became public that American officials, despite their endlessly optimistic public assessments, knew the situation was as bad as Tran had described that day on *Face the Nation*.

As the war expanded and more and more Americans were sent there, Vietnam came to dominate *Face the Nation* as it did other news broadcasts. In 1967, half the programs that *Face the Nation* broadcast were devoted to Vietnam. What is so stunning decades later is not that the war commanded so much attention but how often the people who appeared on *Face the Nation* made statements that would prove so wrong.

Ten weeks after Tran appeared on *Face the Nation* in 1963, Roger Hillsman, the assistant secretary of state for Far Eastern affairs, became the first U.S. government official invited to appear on the broadcast to discuss Vietnam. (In 1959, Senator Homer Capehart, a member of the Senate Foreign Relations Committee, was questioned about Vietnam, but the focus of that broadcast was corruption in the military aid program, not policy.)

Hillsman's appearance would become a template for the scores of administration cabinet officers, military experts, and congressional officials who would appear on the broadcast with rosy predictions and explanations of why news that looked so bad was actually good.

Vietnam remained in turmoil after the overthrow of the Diem regime in 1963 as the first in a series of military juntas took control of the government. Hillsman nevertheless reported "a lot of progress" and said it had been "amazing, the wave of popular support for the military committee."

He saw only one real problem: "The danger," he said, "is going to be that the people were so enthusiastic in their support [of the junta] that it is going to be hard for anyone to fulfill all the expectations."

Hillman's interview was the first of many that should have come with a warning label: "When the subject is Vietnam, listen very carefully."

Although Hillsman was optimistic when reporters tried to pin him down about McNamara's prediction that America's military commitment to South Vietnam could be ended in less than two years, he added a caveat: McNamara, he said, had not promised a complete pull-out. What the official communiqué had said was that people "involved in operational tasks" should be able to leave—not the trainers or the advisers or the military aid. Since the American commitment at that point was confined to sending the South Vietnamese military equipment and advisers and trainers, just who Hillsman was talking about removing was not immediately clear.

*Young CBS News correspondent Dan Rather reported from the jungles of Vietnam, but the correspondents' stories did not jibe with the official version being issued by the Pentagon.*

As the situation continued to deteriorate and the American election year of 1964 began, McNamara made another trip to Vietnam and reported new signs of progress. So it was only natural that when Secretary of State Dean Rusk appeared on *Face the Nation* in March, he would be asked why the government thought things were getting better. From the transcript:

*RUSK: Well, I think that Secretary McNamara has had a chance to look at the situation on the spot and talk to our leaders there. We also had indications of not only the present vigor and the ability of the present leadership of South Vietnam but also of their plans for the future. And so we have, I think, reasons for believing that this effort can be successful along the lines of the present policy.*

79

With the election looming in November, Lyndon Johnson was trying to keep Vietnam as far out of the news as possible, and when Democratic Senator Hubert Humphrey appeared on *Face the Nation* on August 2, he was careful not to do or say anything that would put him on Johnson's bad side. He had good reason for that. He had emerged as the leading candidate to be Johnson's vice-presidential running mate. Unfortunately for him, there was no way to keep Vietnam out of the news that morning. Several hours earlier, the government had reported that a tiny North Vietnamese patrol boat had fired on a U.S. destroyer in international waters off the Vietnam coast in what would become known as the Gulf of Tonkin incident.

Humphrey said he had been briefed by the State Department but had only the barest details and couldn't add much to what was already known. *Face the Nation* panelist Marquis Childs of the *St. Louis Post-Dispatch* wondered if the attack might mean the United States would have to enlarge its military force there.

He told Humphrey that "yesterday, the South Vietnamese minister of defense said that American combat troops would be necessary in the near future," and asked, "Do you think that's a real possibility?"

Humphrey wasn't about to bite on that one. From the transcript:

*HUMPHREY: No, I really do not think that. We ought to keep in mind that there is a degree of political instability in South Vietnam which is rather inevitable in light of the developments there in the past year, and from time to time there will be spokesmen from South Vietnam—in an effort to bolster their own people's morale—that may be making statements that upset us a bit. This isn't uncommon you know. There may be occasional instances within the U.S. when spokesmen make statements for local consumption that upset people in other parts of the world. We are going through some of that right now.*

Two days later, in a national television address, President Johnson reported another attack on a U.S. ship in the Tonkin Gulf and announced he was ordering a bombing campaign into North Vietnam.

The next day, Johnson would use the attacks to justify asking

Congress to pass the Gulf of Tonkin Resolution, which gave him the authority to take any necessary measures to repel future attacks. It passed with only two dissenting votes—Senators Wayne Morse and Ernest Gruening.

The following Sunday, August 9, Minnesota's Democratic senator, Eugene McCarthy, appeared on *Face the Nation*. McCarthy would become a leading opponent of the war, but he had voted for the resolution. But the questions that day did not center on what had happened in the gulf but on whether McCarthy, like Humphrey, was a likely running mate for LBJ. As Humphrey had done, McCarthy parried those questions, but he did not have much to say—one way or the other—about the extraordinary resolution Congress had just passed on the incident involving the U.S. ships and the North Vietnamese torpedo boats.

Robert Pierpoint, the CBS News White House correspondent, was on the *Face the Nation* panel and asked McCarthy if he had any idea why a North Vietnamese patrol boat would take on the U.S. Navy. From the transcript:

MCCARTHY: *Maybe they were bored. Sometimes they say that is what moves people, especially navies, but I can't go into the psychology of the North Vietnamese navy.*

Passage of the Tonkin resolution caused *Face the Nation* producer Prentiss Childs to conclude it was time to pursue the story more aggressively, and three weeks later, he got a commitment to interview Nguyen Khanh, a South Vietnamese general who had taken control of the government. He flew to Saigon, where he was to be joined by CBS News diplomatic correspondent Marvin Kalb; Kalb's brother, Bernard, a veteran foreign correspondent; *Face the Nation*'s director, Robert Vitarelli; and engineer Charles Beckman.

It would prove to be one of the most hair-raising adventures in the history of *Face the Nation*. Upon arrival, Childs discovered that Khanh had been forced by rioting students to give up power only hours earlier. It was unclear who was in charge of the government, but neither Khanh nor anyone else connected with it was willing to be interviewed.

"I had come halfway 'round the world and had been stiffed," Childs told me 30 years later.

He called Washington and told his coproducer, Ellen Wadley, to find another guest there. The Kalbs and the rest of the CBS contingent were expected later that afternoon at the Caravelle Hotel where Childs was staying, and he dreaded telling them the bad news. With nothing else to do, he decided to leave the hotel and buy his wife a gift before making plans to return home.

He had just crossed the street when he was jarred by an ear-shattering explosion behind him. A bomb had gone off in the hotel. Childs later discovered it had been placed in a broom closet next to his room. As smoke poured from the hotel, Childs's reporter instincts kicked in, and he ran back to the street to get a better view. There, in the tree branches overhead, he saw tatters of his own clothes. His room was a shambles. Two Italian reporters and a Vietnamese woman were hurt in the explosion; the bomb had apparently been planted by an antigovernment rebel. CBS News correspondent Murray Fromson had also been registered in the hotel but was not injured.

The CBS group from Washington arrived later that afternoon.

Robert Vitarelli, the *Face the Nation* director who was part of the group, said, "If the bomb had gone off two hours later we would have all been unpacking."

The whole trip would prove unnerving for the CBS team.

"The mobs that had forced General Khanh to resign as head of the government were in an ugly mood. As we drove back to the airport to leave, we were surrounded at one point by a gang of yelling teenagers.

"Foolishly, I got out of the car to clear the way when a Vietnamese driver who spoke English told me to get back in the car because what the teenagers were yelling was 'that car looks new—let's get it.' "

Producer Childs and his crew returned to Washington unhurt, and in one of those strange twists that became the norm in Vietnam,

General Khanh, the man they had all come to Saigon to interview, made peace with the protesters. By the time their plane landed in Washington, Khanh had been restored to power. He wouldn't last long, but he never granted an interview to *Face the Nation*.

"It was a real mess," Childs told me, "but we all realized on that trip that there are worse things than losing an interview."

That fall, LBJ won the presidency in a landslide over Barry Goldwater after promising he would not send American boys to Vietnam to do the job of Asian boys. Within days of the election, reports began to leak that U.S. officials in Saigon had concluded that the American force in Vietnam would have to be enlarged if the Communists were to be turned back. On the weekend after the election, Johnson's national security adviser, McGeorge Bundy, appeared on *Face the Nation*. He wouldn't rule an escalation of the war in or out but told the interviewers, "We are working the problem."

On *Face the Nation*'s last broadcast of that year, Oklahoma Democratic Senator Mike Monroney, just back from Vietnam, had more of the reassuring news that Vietnam visitors often brought home. From the transcript:

*MONRONEY: We are training the Vietnamese to win the war . . . we are their*
*coaches. The war in Vietnam is turning our way. We are winning. Everyone*
*except the Americans knows this.*

Two months later, Vietcong guerrillas launched an attack on Pleiku, South Vietnam, and eight Americans were killed. Johnson ordered a new bombing campaign against North Vietnam that would become known as Rolling Thunder. It would continue for three years.

Secretary of State Rusk returned to *Face the Nation* on March 7, 1965. By then, the bombing campaign had been going on for months, but the only American fighters on the ground thus far were the Green Beret Special Forces troops and other Army advisers who were training the South Vietnamese to fight. That changed with an announcement that 3,500 U.S. Marines were being dispatched to

*When* Face the Nation *producer Prentiss Childs went to Saigon to arrange a broadcast, his hotel room was destroyed by a Vietcong bomb. He's smiling because the bomb went off just minutes after he had left the room. (Prentiss Childs Collection)*

Da Nang, in the northern part of South Vietnam, to guard the air-base being used as the launch point for the bombers flying air strikes into North Vietnam.

Rusk was careful to tell the *Face the Nation* panel that the Marines were being sent there for a specific purpose and it was not to track down and fight the Vietcong and the North Vietnamese soldiers in a ground war. As the president had promised during the campaign, that was the job of the South Vietnamese Army. From the transcript:

*SECRETARY RUSK: The purpose of those Marines is to provide local close-in security for the Marines who are already at Da Nang with Hawk [anti-*

84

*aircraft] missiles and other American personnel there in connection with air-*
*craft. It is not their mission to engage in pacification operations. The fact that*
*they are going in there will make it possible for South Vietnamese forces who*
*have been responsible for the local close-in defense of Da Nang to undertake*
*those missions themselves.*

With so many American combat fliers committed to the war, *New York Times* reporter Max Frankel asked the obvious question, which led to this exchange:

*FRANKEL: Why don't we send some of our ground troops into combat?*
*RUSK: Well, as a matter of fact, the South Vietnamese themselves have felt*
*that ground combat personnel is not what is needed. They have a very sub-*
*stantial armed force that is fighting with effectiveness and with gallantry.*
*There is a problem about foreign ground forces undertaking the kind of*
*pacification effort that is required in South Vietnam. Therefore, we have*
*felt that we should supplement, advise, do things which the South Viet-*
*namese cannot do for themselves. But the South Vietnamese government has*
*not asked for international ground forces to support their effort in South*
*Vietnam.*

As Rusk spoke, administration advisers were already making preparations to expand the war, and within a month, the president
ordered the first ground combat troops into Vietnam. I was a 27-
year-old newspaper reporter for the *Fort Worth Star-Telegram* in
those days, and by the time I arrived in Vietnam in December of
that year, there were nearly 200,000 American troops committed to
Vietnam. The total would rise to 485,000 the next year and go over
a half-million in 1967. Even so, the war never went well. When the
Communists launched the Tet offensive in January 1968 and
demonstrated they could strike at will throughout Vietnam (some
even made it onto the grounds of the U.S. embassy in Saigon),
Johnson's generals asked for even more troops. This was good
news, they said; the Tet offensive had actually been a defeat for the
Communists since they were unable to hold any of the territory

they had attacked. But by then Johnson finally knew better. He turned down the request for more troops and announced he would not seek reelection in order to work full time to end the war through negotiation.

That too failed.

———

# For Want of a Question

## The Pentagon Papers, Gobbledygook and Government Secrecy

*Out of the gobbledygook comes a very clear thing . . . you can't trust the government, you can't believe what they say and you can't rely on their judgment. And, the implicit infallibility of presidents, which has been an accepted thing in America is badly hurt by this because it shows that people do things the President wants to do, even though it's wrong and the President can be wrong.*

Chief of staff H. R. Haldeman explaining the danger
to the Nixon White House caused by the publishing
of the Pentagon Papers, June 14, 1971

Ben Bradlee, the legendary editor of the *Washington Post*, and I share something that both of us would just as soon forget: June 13, 1971, was one of the worst days in our professional lives. Bradlee could see it coming. It took me a day or two to figure it out. Bradlee got scooped that Sunday. I had a major story dropped in my lap and missed it.

It had begun as a lovely, sunny day, and all things considered, official Washington was in a good mood that weekend. The Nixon administration had long since given up hope of winning the Vietnam War and was trying to negotiate a settlement to end it, but there was a bitter fight under way with Congress, which was pressing to set a date certain to bring the troops home. Nevertheless, war casualties were down that weekend, which had buoyed both sides, and as Washington sometimes does, differences were set aside to celebrate the Saturday afternoon wedding of Nixon's older daughter, Tricia. The ceremony had been a glamorous affair at the White House, which had been televised live by all the networks. Even Nixon, no fan of television news, was delighted with the coverage. Thus, when the denizens of official Washington opened their doors that Sunday morning to retrieve their hometown newspaper, Ben Bradlee's *Washington Post*, they couldn't have been too surprised to discover the lead story was not the serious fare they had come to expect from the *Post* but the story of the wedding. It was a happy story. What wedding story isn't? But it gave Bradlee no joy. He had already seen the front page of the *New York Times*, his main competitor. He had been hearing for weeks that the *Times* was about to publish a major scoop, and his people had been unable to find out what it was, the worst feeling an editor can have.

"By that Sunday, I had resigned myself to knowing they had something we didn't have and I just wanted them to publish the thing—whatever it was—so we could get on with following it up," Bradlee told me three decades later.

Now he knew what his competitor had, and it was bigger than he could ever have imagined. Spread across the top of the front page of the *Times* was the first installment of what would be one of the major exclusives in the history of journalism—what came to be called the Pentagon Papers, a 7,000-word top-secret document that detailed the decision-making process of policymakers in the Kennedy and Johnson administrations who had taken the country to war in Vietnam.

"And the front page of my paper—with that story of Tricia Nixon's wedding—looked like a bride's magazine and that just made it worse," Bradlee said.

In truth, the *Times* had also put the Nixon wedding on the front page, but that first installment of the Pentagon Papers was devastating—not just to the *Washington Post*, which had missed the story but to all of the officials of the Johnson and Kennedy administrations because it showed in detail that over the years, again and again, what officials had said in public about the war—the rosy scenarios, the progress reports, the accusations that the press was distorting the story—simply did not jibe with the facts or what the officials themselves had come to believe.

As Nixon's chief of staff, H. R. Haldeman, would tell Nixon the next day, most people would find the report a lot of "gobbledygook." It appeared to deal only with the Kennedy and Johnson administrations, but the politically astute Haldeman saw trouble ahead for the Nixon White House.

"Out of the gobbledygook," he said, "comes a very clear thing . . . you can't trust the government, you can't believe what they say and you can't rely on their judgment. And, the implicit infallibility of presidents, which has been an accepted thing in America is badly hurt by this because it shows that people do things the President wants to do, even though it's wrong and the President can be wrong."

Haldeman and Nixon became convinced that if the person who leaked these massive volumes got away with it, no government secret would be safe. And to be sure, they had plenty of secrets they didn't want the public to know about—foremost among them details of the secret bombing raids that Nixon had ordered into Cambodia in 1969. Many of those details were so closely held that even Nixon's secretaries of defense and state did not know about them at the time.

That Sunday was a bad day for Ben Bradlee, but it should have been a great day for those of us who came to the Washington studios of CBS News that morning to be the questioners on *Face the Nation*, which was scheduled to air at 10:30 A.M. Instead, what happened was one of the most embarrassing Sundays in the history of the broadcast. All this was long before I became the moderator of the broadcast, but I had been invited to join in the questioning because I was the CBS News Pentagon correspondent and our guest that morning was Melvin R. Laird, Nixon's secretary of defense. The Pentagon Papers had been dropped in our lap. In Sunday talk show land, a big story in the Sunday papers is a gift from the news gods because the Sunday broadcasts are the first places for the government officials involved to react. Laird would be the first administration official who had the opportunity to comment on the *Times* story. Whatever he said was bound to make news. Or should have.

Incredibly, we didn't ask him about it. Even visiting reporter John Finney, the Pentagon correspondent for the *New York Times*, didn't bring it up. We had all seen the story that morning, of course, but when Finney and I met before the broadcast with moderator

*When some of the Pentagon Papers were leaked to the press, Nixon's secretary of defense, Melvin R. Laird, thought Nixon should have made all the papers public. But we forgot to ask Laird about it and he kept the information to himself.*

George Herman, we decided the study appeared to focus on previous administrations. Thus, we decided that Laird was not the person to ask about it.

"We thought he was the wrong secretary of defense," Herman remembers thinking. "It didn't seem right to ask Laird about something that happened on McNamara's watch, so we didn't raise it that morning. It was one of the worst mistakes I ever made."

Laird seemed somewhat tense throughout the interview, as if he thought we were setting him up for a question that never came. Once the program concluded, he asked why we had not brought up the story in the *Times*. As he has continued to do over the years, he referred to the study that morning as "the McNamara Papers."

Herman told him what we had decided before the broadcast—that we didn't think he was the right secretary of defense to ask about it.

I can still remember his response:

"Oh?"

Laird and I have become friends over the years and have talked about the incident from time to time, and I wrote about the bonehead mistake in my memoir, *This Just In: What I Couldn't Tell You on TV.* I assumed that if we had asked him that morning, he would have told us that the administration intended to go to court (which it did two days later) in an attempt to stop the *Times* from publishing any more of the study.

As I was in the process of writing this book, I asked Laird if my assumption had been correct.

"Oh hell no," he said. "I came there that morning prepared to tell you that I thought those papers ought to be made public. They were classified top secret, but there were only three or four things in there that should have been classified—we could have excised those things and released the whole thing."

I was stunned because the implications of that were staggering, and Laird certainly must have known it then.

Why did he want to make the study public?

"Because it showed that it was the Kennedy and the Johnson

administrations that had started that war. It laid it out in no uncertain terms that they sent the troops over there and we were the ones who were bringing them home," he said. "During the time I was in Congress, I had become one of the leading critics of how the administration had hidden what was going on there because Johnson's people were trying to conceal how much it was really costing."

(In one of those odd footnotes to history, one of the hardest-hitting speeches that then Congressman Laird made on how the Johnson administration was hiding the cost of war was written by a young college intern named Hillary Rodham. In those days, she was still a Republican, the party of her parents. Later she switched allegiances and became a Democrat. "It was a fine speech," Laird told me. "She was very bright, and I hardly changed a word before I delivered it.")

On that Sunday morning before he appeared on *Face the Nation*, Laird said that he and his top public affairs officers, Daniel Henkin and Jerry Friedheim, had met before the broadcast for breakfast at the Mayflower Hotel near the CBS studio. Henkin and Friedheim had prepared a set of questions they thought Laird would be asked.

"We concluded the entire program would be about that front-page story in the *Times* and nearly all the questions would be about that," he said. "It wasn't the kind of thing I wanted to bring up, but I couldn't believe it when the time rolled by and I was never asked about it."

Clearly that accounted for Laird's uneasiness, but would it have made a difference?

"I don't believe there is any question about that," Laird said. "Two days later, the administration went into court to argue that the national security had been put in danger by release of those papers. It would have been difficult to make that argument if the administration's secretary of defense had already announced on television that he thought the papers ought to be made public."

Neil Sheehan, the *New York Times* reporter who broke the story and wrote the summary of the Pentagon Papers that appeared in the

*Nixon's chief of staff, Al Haig, was the first member of the White House staff to decide that release of the Pentagon Papers posed a danger to Nixon.*

*Times*, believes the implications could have been even wider.

As is now well known, the papers were given to Sheehan by Daniel Ellsberg, a think-tank analyst and a Vietnam veteran who had become a passionate antiwar activist. When the Supreme Court ruled the government had no right to stop the *New York Times* from printing the Pentagon Papers, it was a landmark decision because it reaffirmed the long-standing principle that the government has no right to exercise prior restraint. In lay language, that meant the government could not stop the publication of something in advance, before it was known what that material was.

Newspapers hailed the decision as a victory for the First Amendment, but Nixon's people believed it would open the floodgates— that it would now be virtually impossible for the government to protect legitimate secrets. If the government couldn't stop a newspaper from printing 7,000 pages of material marked top secret, what could the government keep secret? They concluded the only one way to prevent those who disagreed with policy from disclosing secrets was to go after the leaker, Ellsberg. They would make an example of him to show others that such behavior brought with it a severe penalty.

An eccentric former CIA agent named Howard Hunt was brought in to run the operation. He came up with a plan that went far beyond seeking legal charges against Ellsberg. Hunt wanted to ruin him and drew up a detailed plan to smear him—a plan that included breaking into the office of Ellsberg's psychiatrist to collect whatever damaging information about Ellsberg might be found there. The plan was carried out, and the break-in occurred almost a year before Hunt supervised the now-infamous burglary of the Democratic Party headquarters in the Watergate Hotel.

"It makes you wonder," Sheehan told me. "If Laird had said on that broadcast that the Pentagon Papers should have been released, then the administration probably would not have gone to court to try and stop the *Times* from publishing."

If the rest of the Pentagon Papers had then been made public, there would have been no reason to smear Ellsberg, the leaker, or break into his psychiatrist's office. If that break-in had not occurred, would the burglars still have broken in to the Democratic headquarters at the Watergate? Would there have been a Watergate scandal?

"It's a question to ponder," Sheehan said.

Our panel's failure to ask Laird about the Pentagon Papers that Sunday morning was inexcusable—I still can't believe we didn't ask that question—but we could take some consolation in the fact that we were not alone in missing the significance of the story. Richard Nixon missed it at first too.

Nixon said later that he saw the story when he glanced at the front page of the *Times* that Sunday morning but didn't read it. Understandably, the story he read was the account of his daughter's wedding.

Tapes of Nixon's telephone conversations that day have been assembled by the National Security Archive web site, and they show that in the beginning, Nixon did not seem all that upset about the papers being published. Alexander Haig, Henry Kissinger's military assistant, was the first to mention the publication during a midday telephone call. Haig called the leak a "devastating security breach" but didn't bring it up until the end of a conversation that had been mostly about the report that casualties in Vietnam were down. Only when Nixon asked if there was anything else going on did Haig mention the Pentagon Papers. Nixon replied he hadn't read the story.

Secretary of State Rogers called later that afternoon, but they talked mostly about Tricia's wedding. When publication of the papers finally came up, Nixon remarked that from what he had heard, they "were hard on Johnson and Kennedy" but again seemed unconcerned.

It was not until a 3:00 P.M. call from national security adviser Kissinger that Nixon's attitude began to change. When Kissinger told him he "was certain that this violates all sorts of laws," Nixon said, "People have gotta be put to the torch for this sort of thing." At a meeting the next day, Nixon was ready to take action. It was at that meeting that Haldeman had said most people would see the report as "gobbledygook," but that it would "leave people with the impression that the government couldn't be trusted and that people do things the president wants to do even though it's wrong."

Haldeman had correctly foreseen the political impact of publishing the Pentagon Papers. Remarkably, instead of taking his analysis as a warning, Nixon and his people (including Haldeman) took it as a directive. Haldeman has said that the public would take the report to mean that presidents didn't always follow the law and when they asked people to break the law for them, there were always people willing to do it. In an effort to smear Ellsberg, Nixon's people showed that they were willing to do just that, because that is what the president had asked of them. Had they chosen instead to heed Haldeman's warning, perhaps Nixon's presidency would have been saved.

Even before the Supreme Court ruled the administration had no right to bar the *New York Times* from publishing the Pentagon Papers, it was clear the documents were a secret that would not hold. After the courts had temporarily stopped the *Times* from publishing the papers, Ellsberg gave them to the *Washington Post*, which printed another portion of them the next day. The *Boston Globe* soon followed by printing more from the documents, and when the administration tried to stop those newspapers from publishing them, additional chapters from the papers began showing up in newspapers across the country, including the staid *Christian Science Monitor.*

Nixon's people managed to get Ellsberg indicted, but when the judge in that trial learned that Nixon's agents had broken into Ellsberg's psychiatrist's office, he dismissed the case and Ellsberg went free.

We missed the Pentagon Papers story that first Sunday, but we learned our lesson. The next three *Face the Nation* broadcasts were devoted exclusively to the Pentagon Papers and the significance of their disclosure.

Then the story cooled. Within a year, Nixon would go to China and open new arms control initiatives with the Soviets. What we didn't know was that behind the scenes, his people had embarked on the extraordinary plan to close off news leaks that would eventually lead to the unraveling of his presidency. None of that would become known until the summer of 1972, as Nixon was preparing to seek reelection. When the Watergate burglars were arrested, George McGovern, the Democratic presidential candidate, tried to make an issue of it but failed, and Nixon won reelection in a landslide.

Ben Bradlee and his newspaper had been scooped on the Pentagon Papers, but the *Post* and two of its young reporters, Bob Woodward and Carl Bernstein, broke the bigger story of Watergate.

In August 1974, facing certain impeachment and removal from office, Nixon resigned, his top aides went to jail and Gerald Ford became president. Would any of it have happened if we had asked Mel Laird that Sunday about the Pentagon Papers?

"Who knows?" Ben Bradlee mused more than three decades later. "But it would have made my life a lot easier in those weeks after we got scooped."

———◆———

# Badgering George Shultz

## The Rise of Women in
## Politics and Journalism

*Please don't throw me into that ol' briar patch.*

Br'er Rabbit

During the Ford administration, Tom Brokaw, Barbara Walters and I were scheduled to have a group interview with the president. Barbara, who is nothing if not meticulous about preparing for interviews, asked Tom and me to meet with her to talk about how to approach the session.

We met at her New York apartment one Saturday morning and mapped out the areas that should be covered. As we were leaving, she said, "I envy both of you. You can ask tough questions and people say you're tough reporters. But when a woman asks the tough ones, she gets accused of being a 'pushy cookie.'" A "pushy cookie"? The more I thought about it, the more I thought she was probably right.

Until Barbara Walters came along, there had not been many female interviewers, and viewers were unaccustomed to women who posed pointed questions. Somehow that did not fit into a "lady-like" image, and it made viewers uncomfortable.

Make no mistake, it never bothered Walters to ask the questions the rest of us shied away from. During a trip to India with President Carter, she asked Indian Prime Minister Morarji Desai about reports that he drank his own urine.

He readily admitted that he did, bragged on its medicinal qualities and she had a story the rest of us had been too timid to pursue. (For the record, Desai lived into his 90s.)

Although viewers often held women to a different standard than male reporters on television, there have always been women in journalism. But they were seldom in front-line jobs. In the years before television, they were usually feature writers assigned to write for the society page. The hard news was left to the men.

To be sure, the Washington press corps had its occasional female "character." A Maine newspaperwoman named Mae Craig whose trademark was a large flowered hat often provoked news at John Kennedy's news conferences, but more often her offbeat questions produced laughter. Crusty Sara McClendon, who worked for a chain of Texas newspapers, could drive Lyndon Johnson to distraction with some of her questions, but along with the tireless longtime wire service reporter Helen Thomas, they were rarities in a male-dominated profession. As late as 1969, when I arrived in Washington, the Washington press corps was still overwhelmingly white and male. For years, the CBS Washington Bureau had limited itself to one woman in the correspondent ranks and one female editor on the desk. With the coming of the women's movement, the networks came under intense government pressure to hire women, and they were among the first industries to recruit them. Lesley Stahl, who earned her stripes as a rookie reporter in the CBS News Washington Bureau during Watergate, was part of the wave of reporters who came into television during that period. Stahl and her contemporaries got the long-deserved chance to compete with the men and made the most of it. They were as smart, resourceful and as tough as their male competitors.

By the time Stahl was named moderator of *Face the Nation* in 1986, no one thought of her as a "pushy cookie" but as one "tough cookie" who could strike fear in the hearts of presidents and lowly bureaucrats alike. I say that as a compliment.

Of all the moderators who have headed *Face the Nation*, none asked more pointed questions than Stahl. Her interviewing style was as subtle as a runaway bus coming at you head-on, and because of it she sometimes got answers that others didn't.

When I get the runaround from someone I'm interviewing, my usual technique is to approach the same question from another angle or cite facts that raise questions about the veracity of what has just been said. Stahl was more likely to cut to the chase by saying, "That isn't so!" Then she would add the facts and the figures to prove it.

Roderick Townley of *TV Guide* called her the "toughest of the Sunday morning interviewers."

"Essentially, she'll shoot at anything that moves, on the left or the right," he said. "She is first and foremost a watch dog with perhaps a streak of pit bull somewhere in her ancestry."

Even so, Stahl herself sometimes worried about being too aggressive. But she never pushed harder than she did during an interview with Secretary of State George Shultz in 1986—one of my favorite stories and one of her biggest scoops. First, the background:

Ronald Reagan had cut taxes and begun a military buildup during his first term and won reelection in a landslide, but midway into his second term, his administration seemed to be falling apart. Suddenly one of America's most popular presidents found himself mired in a scandal that became known as Iran-contra.

Agents of Reagan, the president who had stood tall against terrorists, had been caught trading arms with the terrorist state of Iran in return for a promise to free some of the American hostages Iran was holding.

It was not only a dubious plan but clearly illegal: Reagan himself had signed a law banning such transactions. And that was only part it. It was being run out of the White House National Security Council without the knowledge of either Secretary of State Shultz or Secretary of Defense Caspar Weinberger. The two secretaries thought the plan not only illegal but stupid, and once they discovered what was going on, they tried to shut it down—but to no avail: they could not convince the president that he was violating the law.

As top-level officials argued behind the scenes, White House aides little known to the public, Admiral John Poindexter and an adventurous Marine lieutenant colonel named Oliver North, were not only shipping illegal arms to Iran but overcharging the Iranians and using the profits to fund another operation—contra forces fighting rebels in Central America.

The president made matters worse when he went on television and admitted some arms had been shipped to Iran but denied that he was trading with an admitted terrorist state.

*Lesley Stahl, one of* Face the Nation's *toughest questioners, covered the White House during the week and anchored* Face the Nation *on Sundays.*

"We did not—repeat—did not trade weapons or anything else for hostages, nor would we," the president declared.

Few believed him, and as Stahl said later, "The White House needed credibility so they all but forced a reluctant Shultz to appear on one of the Sunday shows. He chose *Face the Nation.*"

That would prove to be a mistake for the White House. It was well known that Shultz opposed sending arms to Iran, and Stahl lost no time in asking him why.

"We need to respond to terrorism," Shultz told her, "and among our responses is our denial of arms shipments to Iran. That policy remains our policy. It is in effect, and there it is."

Stahl was stunned. She would later recall that she had said to herself, *What does that mean? We sent arms but we have a policy not to send arms.*

Was the secretary of state publicly admonishing the president, who had confirmed on television that arms had indeed been shipped?

At one point she said, "I don't want to badger you, but you are not answering my question."

That brought perhaps the most unusual response ever given by a person being questioned on *Face the Nation.*

"Well, no, you can badger me," he said.

Even Stahl was taken aback. "Why did you—okay, good," she stammered. "Why did you not tell the Arabs the truth?"

As Shultz later wrote in his own book, *Turmoil and Triumph: My Years as Secretary of State,* "I wanted to set straight where I stood . . ."

And for sure, he did.

"It is clearly wrong to trade arms for hostages. So that is our policy. . . . It isn't the right thing for governments to trade arms or anything else for hostages, just because it encourages taking more," he said.

Stahl asked if there would be more arms shipments.

"It is certainly against our policy," Shultz responded.

"That's not an answer," Stahl said. "Why don't you answer the question directly? I'll ask it again: Will there be any more arms shipments to Iran, either directly by the United States or through any third parties?"

"Under the circumstances of Iran's war with Iraq, in pursuit of terrorism, its association with those holding our hostages, I would certainly say, as far as I'm concerned, no," Shultz answered.

That was when Stahl came back with a follow-up question that deserves to be in the Interviewing Hall of Fame.

"Do you have the authority," she asked, "to speak for the entire administration?"

Shultz's reply was as quick as it was startling.

"No," he replied. And on that word the interview ended.

It was the kind of performance almost never seen in Washington. A top cabinet officer had gone on television and in effect had rebuked the president of the United States for violating his own policy. The next day, it made front-page headlines in hundreds of papers around the United States and other countries as well.

It also brought down the wrath of many in the administration—including the First Lady—on George Shultz, but he was a man of honor and he had refused to lie. In the end, he won.

As Shultz later wrote, "The next day the White House blinked." Reagan's spokesman, Larry Speakes, issued a statement saying, "Shultz *did* speak for the administration" and "the president has no desire, the president has no plans, to send further arms to Iran."

Shultz had accomplished on *Face the Nation* what he had been unable to do within the inner councils of the government: shut down an illegal operation and regained control of American foreign policy.

Sometimes a little badgering can be the start of something grand.

The collapse of Soviet communism came on Stahl's shift as moderator of *Face the Nation*, and because she was also the White House correspondent, many of the *Face the Nation* broadcasts originated overseas or wherever else the president might be traveling, which presented daunting technical challenges.

During an arms control negotiation in Geneva, she got an exclusive interview with Reagan's chief of staff, Don Regan, only to learn the broadcast had been beamed back to the United States minus pictures. Even so, ratings for the broadcast were about the same as always. The usual number of loyal *Face the Nation* viewers had tuned in to "watch" what was essentially a radio broadcast.

A meeting between Soviet leader Mikhail Gorbachev and Reagan's successor, George H. W. Bush, held just off the island of Malta provided another logistical nightmare. Bush wanted the meetings to take place on ship rather than on shore. A storm packing winds that Dan Rather said "would have driven Sinbad the Sailor and Lord Nelson to cover" swept the area and almost wrecked the entire session. The weather was so bad that it overshadowed what was going on at the summit. At one point as the president was trying to get ashore in a small launch after a meeting aboard one of the larger ships, the waves got so high that Secret Service agents could be seen holding the president tightly to keep him from being swept overboard.

Secretary of State James Baker said the American delegation had worn antiseasick patches in order to continue negotiations. Why they didn't just move the talks to buildings on the mainland was never explained.

A big wind would later produce one of the daffiest scenes ever recorded on *Face the Nation*. Stahl, in Washington, had lined up a satellite interview in Moscow with Gorbachev's spokesman, Gennadi Gerasimov, who was standing in front of Saint Basil's Cathedral in Red Square. As the interview began, a heavy rain blew suddenly into Moscow. As Stahl began to ask about a letter that Gorbachev had recently received from Bush, Gerasimov began wrestling with a huge umbrella. As the interview progressed, Gerasimov's comb-over flew straight up and remained vertical, as if called to attention. Stahl recalled that she was concerned the Russian "would just lift off under that umbrella like Mary Poppins."

Stahl handled such moments with aplomb, but handling weather emergencies was not where she left her mark. It was her ability to come up with a tough question that caused her to be seen as one of the best of the new reporters who also happened to be women.

She went up against some of the most difficult people in the world to interview and held her own with the best of them. In one famous encounter (a rare taped interview rather than a live broadcast) with Yasir Arafat, she accomplished the near impossible. She brought Arafat's trademark filibusters to a dead stop when she shouted, "This is not a *speech show*, and it is a *Q and A show*. You must let me ask you a question!"

"Oh pardon, lady," he responded. But when she asked him why he wasn't encouraging a home-grown leadership that the Israelis were willing to deal with, he asked her if she was a spokesman for the Israeli government.

Stahl told him she didn't believe attacking her would get him anything and suggested he answer the question. He did, at least as directly as Arafat ever answered a question.

As I have reviewed the tapes and transcripts of *Face the Nation* broadcasts over these past 50 years, one thing that has struck me is how these broadcasts have documented the changing role of women in journalism and in politics. When I began as a reporter back in the 1950s, it would have been unheard of to send a woman reporter to do an interview with a Yasir Arafat (too dangerous) or even a George Shultz (too intimidating). Someone would have blocked it, believing that such important figures would not take a woman interviewer seriously.

The Barbara Walterses and the Helen Thomases taught us better, of course, and the wave of women who came after them during the 1970s—the group that included Lesley Stahl and Diane Sawyer—validated what Barbara and Helen had shown us. These were reporters who could handle whatever came their way.

The same could be said for the women on the other side of the table—the growing number of women who were coming into politics or serving in the government.

The first women did not appear on *Face the Nation* until its second anniversary broadcast, when Eleanor Roosevelt and Maine Sen-

*On November 4, 1956,* Face the Nation's *second anniversary, former first lady Eleanor Roosevelt and Maine Senator Margaret Chase Smith became the first women to appear on the broadcast.*

ator Margaret Chase Smith appeared to comment on Eisenhower's reelection campaign against Adlai Stevenson.

When I arrived in Washington in 1969, Senator Smith was still the only woman in that august body. Now there are 14, as well as 62 women in the House of Representatives. The Democratic leader in the House is a woman, Nancy Pelosi of California. In three states— California, Washington and Maine—both senators were women in 2004. Women now play key roles throughout the government. President Bush's national security adviser is a woman, and women hold key assignments throughout his administration, as they did during President Clinton's two terms.

Equality has come to mean that female correspondents are no longer considered "unladylike" for asking tough questions. Nor do women who hold positions in the government expect special treatment. We ask them the same questions we would ask a man. Gender does not figure into it.

Lesley Stahl will be happy to tell you she ran up against no one tougher than British Prime Minister Margaret Thatcher. During a 1987 appearance on *Face the Nation*, she pressed the "Iron Lady" for an answer, only to be instructed, "You may go on asking the same question 100 different ways and you will still get the same answer."

George Herman also cited a woman, Israeli Prime Minister Golda Meir, as one of the toughest people he ever interviewed. After one broadcast, she scolded Herman for asking too many questions about a Lebanese airliner that had been forced down by Israeli

*With the coming of the women's movement, women became an important part of* Face the Nation *as questioners and guests. Moderator George Herman called Israeli Prime Minister Golda Meir one of the toughest people he had ever interviewed, "man or woman."*

fighter planes. "Too many questions about that damn airliner," she said as she got up after the broadcast.

"She just kept saying it over and over," Herman said, "I walked her out to the curb where a dozen or so people were waiting to see her and she waved and smiled but as she got into the car and sat down, she looked up at me and said it again, 'Too damn many questions about that plane.' "

Meir was a chain smoker, and after the broadcast she noticed that producer Sylvia Westerman smoked filter tips. She told her she needed to smoke stronger ones if she wanted to relax.

Women will argue there is still a way to go to achieve full equality, and as the father of two women and the grandfather of two more, I urge them to keep pushing. But to understand how our perception of women and their role in politics and journalism has changed, I offer portions of the *Face the Nation* broadcast of February 2, 1964, when the guest was Senator Margaret Chase Smith, who had just announced she was running for the Republican presidential nomination, the first woman in American history to seek the presidential nomination of either major party.

After quizzing Senator Smith about the historic aspects of her bid and whether she really thought she had a chance, panelist Warren Dufee, the Senate correspondent for United Press International, asked why she felt she was "better qualified than any one of the several men who are also seeking the nomination?"

The senator responded that she had been in the House and Senate for 23 years, had missed only one vote since 1955 and simply felt she had a greater list of accomplishments than any of the other announced candidates.

Then it was CBS News correspondent George Herman's turn. From the transcript:

MR. HERMAN: *Senator Smith, not all countries have the same attitude toward women as the U.S. How do you think a woman president in the U.S. would make out in international conferences and those so-called nose-to-nose meetings?*

*SENATOR SMITH: Well, I would remind you that that there was once a Joan of Arc. I would remind you that once there was a Catherine the Great. I would remind you that there was a Queen Victoria. I would also call attention to Mr. Khrushchev's references to me through the years, when he called me an "Amazon warmonger hiding behind a rose." The press over there called me a cannibalistic little lady.*

Referring to former Vice President Nixon's famous kitchen debate with Khrushchev, moderator Paul Niven asked:

*MR. NIVEN: How do you think you would make out in a kitchen confrontation with Mr. Khrushchev?*
*SENATOR SMITH: Well, I wouldn't care to estimate that. If it was making blueberry muffins, I probably would win.*

Senator Smith was a member of three of the Senate's most important committees—Space, Armed Services and Appropriations—but as time was running out, moderator Niven ended the program this way. From the transcript:

*MR. NIVEN: Senator, to end on a lighter note, would you, if elected the first woman president—redecorate the White House?*
*SENATOR SMITH: Well, I haven't looked the White House over and I wouldn't, I couldn't answer that because I have been told that it has been done pretty well by Mrs. Kennedy and Mrs. Johnson.*
*MR. NIVEN: And would you appoint any men to your cabinet?*
*SENATOR SMITH: You didn't see my cabinet proposals last year did you?*
*MR. NIVEN: I did. Well thank you very much Senator Smith, for joining us on* Face the Nation.

It would take a brave (and foolish) soul to pose such questions to the women who sit in the Senate and House chambers today.

# The Sunday Primaries
## Tales from the Campaign Trail

*Go vote! It will make you feel big and strong!*

The author, election eve 2000

I love politics, so it will come as no surprise that my favorite stories about *Face the Nation* have usually come from our political broadcasts. In presidential politics especially, *Face the Nation* has always played an important role. Candidates have used the program to launch campaigns and to end them—sometimes on purpose, sometimes not.

Alabama Governor George Wallace had threatened to run in 1964, but when Barry Goldwater got the Republican nomination, Wallace came on *Face the Nation* to say he had achieved his goal of "conservatizing" both parties and folded his campaign.

That same year, Pennsylvania Governor William Scranton wrecked his presidential campaign on *Face the Nation* with a performance so wobbly that he was no longer taken seriously as a candidate.

In 1972, Missouri Senator Tom Eagleton appeared on *Face the Nation* to explain why he had not disclosed he had been treated for mental illness before McGovern picked him as his running mate.

After the questioners had spent most of the broadcast talking about Eagleton's mental state, McGovern realized the issue would never go away. The next day, he announced that Eagleton would be leaving the ticket.

The Sunday talk shows are made for politics. They are not places for investigative journalism or long, in-depth feature stories. They are places where candidates can be questioned directly and at some length about their positions on the issues during live, unedited interviews.

My competitor Tim Russert had it right when he once told me, "What we do is not complicated; we turn on the studio lights and ask questions."

Therein lies the value of these broadcasts.

Candidates appear on them knowing they'll get tough, no-nonsense questions, but they also know that if they do well, they'll gain stature in the eyes of voters. The Sunday broadcasts have become such important stops on the campaign trail that the candidates call them the "Sunday primaries." In the summer of 2003, we began coverage of the coming campaign by inviting the likely candidates to be interviewed. I asked a key Democrat if he thought the early interviews were all that important since most Americans were not yet focused on politics.

"Oh yes," he said. "Most Americans are not focused on primaries but the political community—the people who give money, the political consultants, the party activists—are already looking for a horse, for someone to back. How these candidates do on these early Sunday shows has a tremendous impact on those people. It's a long journey to any nomination, but the first step for a candidate is convincing the political community that he or she has the stuff to slug it out on Sunday. The shows really are important in that sense."

I have always believed that the most successful politicians in every era have been those who mastered the dominant media of their day. In colonial America, the world got most of its news by printed word, and that remarkable group of men we know as the founding fathers were all writers of exceptional skill.

*Gerald Ford was the first sitting president to appear on* Face the Nation. *His 32-year-old chief of staff, Dick Cheney, later George W. Bush's vice president, is in the striped shirt. Moderator Herman is at far left. Bureau chief Sanford Socolow is to Cheney's right.*

As radio became the place where more and more Americans got their news, Franklin Roosevelt became the first politician to recognize its power and how to use it. Until then, most politicians and even some newscasters addressed the radio audience as if they were making a speech to a large crowd. Roosevelt was the first politician to understand it wasn't the same. Radio was a personal medium. It was like a friend who had come to visit. Families gathered in their living rooms around their radios. Roosevelt had the imagination to see those families sitting there, and he spoke to them in a quiet, calm voice as if he were a friend who had come to call. Thus his fireside chats were born, a technique copied by hundreds of politicians who came after him, but a technique never mastered in the way Roosevelt had. Roosevelt used the fireside chats so effectively that a British newspaper suggested that Ramsey MacDonald and Stanley Baldwin, the colorless British parliamentary leaders, might try the same approach, which led Winston Churchill to quip, "If they tried it, the fire would go out."

The first and most successful politician of the television age was John Kennedy who was—not surprisingly—the first to understand the power of the new medium and how to use it.

Until Kennedy took office, no president had ever allowed one of his news conferences to be broadcast live. Eisenhower allowed the sessions to be filmed, but they were not broadcast until the transcripts had been reviewed by Eisenhower's press secretary, James C. Hagerty. Broadcasting a president's unscripted remarks live was thought too dangerous. What if the president made a slip? What if he inadvertently said something that insulted the Soviet Union and set off a nuclear war? Kennedy thought that view was nonsense. He saw no risk. He had been dealing with the press all his life, enjoyed it and considered himself up to answering whatever questions might come his way.

When Kennedy's news conferences were broadcast live, the events themselves became news. Suddenly Americans had access to more than just what he said. They could take the measure of a politician, how he looked. Was he nervous? Confident? In the case of Kennedy, a man of charm and wit, that fuller measure was all to his advantage. His confident air was as important to shaping his favorable image as were the answers he gave. What Kennedy and his people grasped before others did was that communicating in the television age is more than just the words we speak. It is how we speak them, and sometimes where we speak them, that shapes the perception people have of us. Ronald Reagan once wrote that the only image most people have of themselves is the one they see in the mirror when they shave. But the Old Actor knew that others don't always see us in a close-up. Their perception of us comes from seeing us in wide shots as well—when they subconsciously judge us by how we walk, by our posture and demeanor. Much of Reagan's success as a communicator resulted from the fact that he "looked like a president." Reagan and his aides understood that.

Reagan's aide Mike Deaver used to say, "You never saw a bad picture of Ronald Reagan." He was right, and it was no accident.

Television was not much of a factor in presidential politics until the 1960 campaign, and Kennedy used it extensively. He appeared four times on *Face the Nation*, and the ease with which he handled a sensitive question about his religion on a *Face the Nation* broadcast, on the eve of the Wisconsin primary, showed his early mastery of the medium.

Wisconsin counted many Catholics among its voters, and questioner Peter Lisagor of the *Chicago Daily News* wanted to know if

*John Kennedy was among the first politicians to recognize the power of television. He appeared on* Face the Nation *early in his Senate career.*

Kennedy intended to solicit Catholic votes. It was almost a trick question, since Kennedy's Catholicism had been an issue throughout the campaign and he had vowed to steer clear of orders from the Vatican.

*LISAGOR: Do you think there is a Catholic voting bloc in the state of Wisconsin?*
*KENNEDY: No. I think I have stated on many occasions that I hoped that no one would vote for me because I was Catholic or against me because I was Catholic. There are a great many serious issues facing the United States. Where I went to church this morning, Sunday, seems to be really important only to me. And I would hope that with all the matters that face the United States, that we would want, certainly, to discuss all those questions which go to the survival of this country without really worrying about my religion. The Constitution took care of this matter most satisfactorily. The First Amendment and the separation of church and state, Article Six, which says there shall be no religious test for office—that is what I believe. And that, in my opinion is what the majority of the citizens of Wisconsin believe.*

To see those words in print tells only part of the story. Kennedy appeared confident and comfortable with himself as he answered the question, and his demeanor could not help but convey a feeling of reassurance to those worried about "Vatican control" over the president.

Richard Nixon had appeared on *Face the Nation* in previous years as both a senator and vice president, but he never appeared during that campaign year, which probably hurt him. When Kennedy bested him in the famously remembered debates late in the campaign, there can be little doubt that Kennedy's familiarity with the medium, honed by the give-and-take on broadcasts such as *Face the Nation*, gave him a decided advantage in a race that he won by one of the closest margins ever.

Lyndon Johnson hated television as much as Kennedy loved it. Johnson understood the power of TV (and its economic value—he owned the only television station in Austin, Texas), but he also understood he was not very good at it. Johnson was the consummate dealmaker and, off camera, one of the most impressive men I ever met or tried to interview. But on television, he came off as corny, conniving and uncomfortable. It bothered him that he didn't know what to do about it, but he avoided television interviews when he could, and during his time as president he never appeared on *Face the Nation*.

Arizona Senator Barry Goldwater, who challenged Johnson for the presidency in 1964, had just the opposite problem: he was too comfortable on TV, so relaxed he was likely to say whatever crossed his mind. Goldwater was one of the most outspoken members of the Senate. He once remarked that the country would be better off if the eastern seaboard could somehow be sawed off and allowed to float out to sea. Another time, he suggested lobbing a nuclear bomb "into the men's room of the Kremlin." Goldwater's candor could be refreshing, even funny, and such remarks were generally not taken seriously until he became a presidential candidate. After that, the loose talk frightened voters.

During one interview on *Face the Nation*, he said it was time to return to nuclear brinksmanship—the policy of threatening to use nuclear weapons to achieve our foreign policy objectives. From the transcript:

*ROGER MUDD: Don't you run a pretty terrible risk, going right up to the brink in this day and age with such weapons as both sides possess?*
*SENATOR GOLDWATER: Well, let's go back to the Eisenhower-Dulles days; this was the period in our recent history when we had more secure peace than we have had since. Under Eisenhower and Dulles, brinkmanship was used at Formosa, it was used in Lebanon, it was used in many places and we didn't become engaged in war. We are engaged in a war in South Vietnam now that is not a guerrilla war anymore, it is an out and out war, and that is not escalating into any holocaust. I think the only way we are going to keep peace in the world is to make our enemies certain that we will go so far and we will tolerate no more.*

Forty years later, a reader still asks himself, "Did he really say that?" He did.

115

Johnson was no master of television, but when your opponent advocates threatening nuclear war as the solution to solving foreign policy problems, you don't have to do many television interviews yourself.

It was Pennsylvania Governor William Scranton's short-lived campaign for the presidency that turned out to be one of the strangest stories of 1964, and it played out on *Face the Nation* one Sunday in June. To the chagrin of East Coast Republicans, it was beginning to look as if Goldwater, the darling of the right, would soon have a lock on the presidential nomination unless someone could be found to oppose him. The moderate Scranton emerged as the likely choice to block Goldwater, and the week before he was to appear on *Face the Nation*, former President Eisenhower asked him to drop by his Gettysburg farm for a chat. Scranton left the meeting

*In 1980, Jimmy Carter became the second sitting president to appear on the broadcast. (l–r) Moderator George Herman, AP reporter Walter Mears, correspondent Lesley Stahl and CBS News president Bill Leonard.*

believing he had Eisenhower's endorsement and backing to seek the nomination. Without his backing, Scranton knew, he had no chance against Goldwater. With it, he decided, there was a chance he could stop Goldwater and get the nomination for himself. Before he came to *Face the Nation* that morning, he wrote out a statement announcing his candidacy, brought it with him to the studio and placed it face down on the table. At some point in the broadcast, he had planned to read it. The reporters had been tipped that Scranton would make news and eyed the paper on the table before him. But when they questioned him, he bobbed and weaved and refused to say what he might do. He said he would be "available" for the nomination. What did that mean? Scranton wouldn't say.

It was an odd performance. Scranton had come off as indecisive, nervous, even downright strange. George Herman had been on the panel that day and was as puzzled as the other reporters. What the reporters didn't know was that as Scranton was leaving for the studio that morning, he had received an unexpected call from Eisenhower. The old general wanted to make sure that Scranton understood that he was not endorsing him, only encouraging him. Further, Ike said he could not be part of any "block Goldwater" movement. Had Scranton misunderstood his original conversation with Eisenhower? Had someone convinced Ike to change his mind? The answer has never surfaced, but for whatever reason, Eisenhower was not supporting Scranton as Scranton had believed, and he was devastated by the news. It is little wonder, then, that Scranton had appeared visably shaken when he appeared later to answer reporters' questions on *Face the Nation*.

He had entered the studio planning to announce a presidential campaign. He had left with reporters shaking their heads in wonderment. Scranton eventually announced his candidacy, but he never shook the indecisive, odd impression that he had left that day on the *Face the Nation* broadcast, and his campaign went nowhere.

If possible, the 1972 appearance of Democratic candidate George McGovern's running mate, Tom Eagleton, was even stranger than Scranton's—more than strange, because it was also a lesson in the hard, cold reality of practical politics. Eagleton came to the broadcast the week after news had broken that he had once been given shock treatments and was still taking medication for mental illness. Inexplicably, Eagleton had not told McGovern about his illness when McGovern asked him to be his running mate, and the news had touched off a firestorm.

Eagleton came to *Face the Nation* that Sunday to answer the critics and to say that he intended to remain on the ticket. Further, he had talked to McGovern and still enjoyed his support. What Eagleton had not known was that McGovern's handpicked choice to head the Democratic National Committee, Jean Westwood, had gone on *Meet the Press* opposite Eagleton that morning to send an obvious signal. She said he should step down and allow McGovern to choose someone else.

It was hot in the CBS studio that day, and that led to another bizarre turn in the interview: Eagleton began to sweat profusely. Moderator George Herman knew Eagleton had a tendency to perspire under the TV lights, and since he was being questioned about his mental state, Herman thought he should give him a chance to explain that the beads of sweat forming on his face were perfectly normal for him.

"I had heard him joke about it and say, 'The Eagleton family can sweat in a snow storm,'" Herman remembered, "so I asked him why he was perspiring so profusely but he didn't make light of it; he just said he was fine."

Herman had wanted to give Eagleton a chance to explain, but the question had not come out the way he had intended. Viewers were outraged. Herman got hundreds of letters of protest.

After watching the broadcast, McGovern decided Eagleton had to be replaced, and the next day he stepped down. John Kennedy's brother-in-law, Sargent Shriver, would be named to take his place.

"I really felt badly for Eagleton," Herman said. "But when he heard I was being criticized for asking him about sweating, he wrote me a letter to say he had no problem with it and that he had not been upset with me for asking.

"He was a real gentleman and I'll always remember it."

• • •

All of the men who have served as president since Eisenhower have appeared on *Face the Nation,* but only three of them—Gerald Ford, Jimmy Carter and Bill Clinton—have appeared on the broadcast while in office.

Ford and Carter appeared as they were campaigning for new terms, and Clinton appeared midway into his second term (before the Monica Lewinsky story broke).

As the White House correspondent during Ford's two years as the nation's first unelected president, I was one of the reporters who questioned him during his visit to *Face the Nation.* It was an interview that produced little news, but I may have set a new standard for asking a long, convoluted question when a shorter one would have served better. From the transcript:

SCHIEFFER: *Mr. President, let me get back just for a moment to Ronald Reagan. One of the most interesting things I think that has been found by the CBS/New York* Times *Poll is a statistic they came up with the other day that said if the race were Ford versus Carter, 41 percent of those who called themselves Reagan people would defect and vote for Jimmy Carter. It also says that 23 percent of those who call themselves Ford voters would defect to Carter if Reagan is the nominee.[Whew!] In light of that, aren't you going to have to put Ronald Reagan on the ticket if you're going to have the backing of your party?*

Luckily Ford had been around Washington long enough not to need a translator.

FORD: *I've said that I would not exclude any Republican that I've looked at or we've heard about that might qualify as being a vice-presidential candidate and that would include Ronald Reagan. Now, he has himself indicated he would not be interested in being vice president but as far as I'm concerned I would not exclude him.*

He did exclude him, of course, and chose Bob Dole. He had no

*It was said that Ronald Reagan never took a bad picture, and that was certainly the case when the Old Actor appeared on the broadcast in 1978.*

intention of rewarding Reagan, the man who had forced him to spend half the year fighting for his own party's nomination when he should have been concentrating on his Democratic opponent.

Carter would become the second sitting president to appear on *Face the Nation*. The interview came in 1980 during his campaign for reelection against Reagan. Under questioning by Lesley Stahl, Carter's appearance underlined that his administration was in such a shambles that even his own people were challenging him publicly. From the transcript:

*STAHL: Mr. President, you keep emphasizing social programs lately and you fought against a proposal in Congress to increase the military budget. You did that even though your Joint Chiefs of Staff took the unusual step of going public in opposition. How can you defend your argument . . . with that kind of opposition? And how can you tolerate the Joint Chiefs exhibiting so much insubordination to you?*

*CARTER: It's not an unprecedented thing . . . During the eight years of Republican administration before I became president, we had a net reduction in real dollars of 30 percent expenditures for defense, 30 percent cut over an eight-year period. I've only been in office now a little over three years and we have had a very good increase—*

*STAHL: But you campaigned—*

*CARTER: We—Do you want me to answer your question?*

*STAHL: Yes, sir. But—*

*CARTER: Okay.*

Bill Clinton had appeared on *Face the Nation* as a candidate in 1991. The interview had gone smoothly, and I had been impressed with his ability to handle complicated questions, but it would be 1997 and well into his second term before he appeared again, this time as a sitting president. The interview had a much different tone from our first session. The Whitewater real estate scandal was in the news, and Susan McDougal, the wife of one of Clinton's former business partners, had been jailed for refusing to tell what she knew about the deal. It led to a sharp confrontation, and America saw a harder, much testier side of Clinton than it had seen in the past. From the transcript:

*SCHIEFFER: Let me ask you one more question about that, and that is regarding Susan McDougal. She's in jail because the prosecutor says she will not cooperate. She will—she did not talk when, apparently, they asked her, "Were you telling the truth?" at her trial. What—many people have said to me, when they knew I was preparing to do this interview, "Ask the president, why doesn't he simply tell Susan McDougal, 'Tell the truth, Susan,' and— and that would take care of it.*

*CLINTON: First of all, that's—that's not what she has said. Secondly, she has a lawyer. She has a lawyer. They know what they're doing. You have to presume that. I mean, I don't know what the facts are. But she has said repeatedly that neither I nor my wife did anything wrong.*

*She has said repeatedly, and said, I believe on your network just the other night, that the other people weren't telling the truth and that if she told the truth, she was afraid she'd be punished for it. Now that's what she said. I think you have to let her and her lawyer decide what they think is in—the right thing to do and do it.*

SCHIEFFER: *So you have no advice for her?*

CLINTON: *I have no comment on it. It's none of my business.*

That would be Bill Clinton's last appearance on *Face the Nation.* In a matter of months, he would become embroiled in the Monica Lewinsky affair and would never again run the risk of appearing on one of the Sunday shows.

By the year 2000, the Sunday shows had become a major—if not the major— battleground for campaign coverage.

The year before, it had become clear that the races would come down to Texas Governor George W. Bush and maverick John McCain on the Republican side and Clinton's vice president, Al Gore, and New Jersey's former senator, Bill Bradley, on the Democratic side.

In October 1999, we had what would prove to be an unusual encounter with Vice President Gore.

Gore's campaign was doing well enough, but he had been struggling to find some way to appear more relaxed and down to earth. Of all the politicians I have covered, I have never known one whose on-camera persona is so different from the way he appears off camera. Gore is smart, witty, a wonderful father—and all that shows off camera. Turn on the lights, and he becomes stiff and uncomfortable—someone who appears to say nothing unless he has rehearsed it in advance.

Gore was in Maine, and we had arranged to interview him on the balcony of a beautiful seaside resort. The Atlantic Ocean would provide the backdrop. Or so we thought. We arrived on a Saturday only to be met by a very young Gore aide who told us she thought the setting too posh—a place where rich people would congregate. Not

*Bill Clinton appeared twice on* Face the Nation, *once as governor and once as president, midway into his second term. Once the Monica Lewinsky story broke, he never again appeared on a Sunday show.*

the setting for Al Gore. We argued that the Atlantic Ocean had a fairly universal appeal, that rich and poor had enjoyed it over the years. But to no avail. It soon became obvious the young woman had been put in charge of something she knew nothing about. We were unable to reach anyone else on Gore's staff, and she was determined to do it her way. She had decided the proper place for the interview would be in front of the vegetable counter at the local public market. We went there and discovered it looked just like what it was: a vegetable counter. To put on a live broadcast from there would require moving half the counters in the rest of the market in order to make room for the cameras and lights. We tried to explain how complicated this was going to be.

"Why?" she wanted to know. "You just put the camera over there." It was then that I understood the woman had apparently never seen a live television broadcast. We were not talking about one camera or a reporter conducting a brief street-corner interview. We were talking about three cameras and studio lights to produce a broadcast that met professional standards. We were talking about laying cables to a remote control truck, satellites, backup lines. It would take us all night to convert this vegetable market into a television studio. Nevertheless, we got it done.

It was going to be a strange setting to talk politics—before a background of pumpkins and squash—but it was not until Gore arrived that we realized that the young campaign aide had apparently done what someone had told her to do. Gore was clearly trying to change his image. I saw him come around the vegetable counter and I thought, "My God, we're in a farmers' market and he's come dressed as a farmer." He wore work pants, an open-collar shirt and work boots. I noticed as he sat and crossed his legs that the sole of his boot appeared totally clean. If he had worn the boots before, he had not worn them often.

It was during this period that Gore's advisers had been telling him to take off the ties and blue suits and switch to beiges and softer colors, which was supposed to make him more an "alpha male"— whatever that was.

The interview went nowhere so I brought up the new look. From the transcript:

SCHIEFFER: *I see you're out of the blue suit, you're out of the tie. Is this the new Al Gore?*
GORE: *No. Well, there are not many people in suits and ties here at the Public Market in Portland, Maine. And I'm—I'm taking the campaign and my candidacy right to the grass roots, and talking with people about how we can create the kind of future that people want to see for their families.*

No, there were not many people there in suits and ties, but there were not many people there to be interviewed on television. It had all been carefully planned and plotted, but it was so different from what we were used to and Gore's answers were so clearly rehearsed that it was all somewhat jarring. After the broadcast, a CBS executive called me from New York and said, "I think there's something wrong with him." I told him I didn't agree; I just thought he was being overadvised, that a new set of advisers had taken over the campaign and had given him bad advice.

On the Republican side, John McCain had appeared on *Face the Nation* several times in 1999, but we never got an interview with George Bush until the Sunday before the New Hampshire primary.

It was a snowy New Hampshire day. We interviewed him from

*Dwight Eisenhower did not appear on* Face the Nation *until after he left the presidency. His one appearance came in 1963, nine days after John Kennedy's State of the Union Address.*

our election headquarters in New Hampshire, and I thought it was one of the best interviews Bush had given throughout the campaign. Bush had been a consensus builder during his two terms as Texas governor, and had often reached out to Democrats to form alliances and pass legislation. That Sunday in New Hampshire, he talked about how he hoped to do the same thing as president. From the transcript:

SCHIEFFER: *Your dad used to say he was the foreign policy president, that was his expertise. What would you say is your area of expertise?*

BUSH: *Uniting people and setting an agenda that is hopeful and optimistic, bringing people together to achieve that agenda. Coming to Washington, D.C., and saying it is important to have an administration with a different attitude. We got to reject zero-sum politics, pitting one group of people against another and elevating the debate so that should I be the nominee, I'm gonna say, "Give me a chance to bring people together to solve Medicare or Social Security. Give me a chance to cut the taxes or give me a chance to strengthen the military." I think America will find I've got the capacity to do that.*

As he left our headquarters, I congratulated him on what I thought had been a fine interview. I thought he had said exactly what needed to be said. Our politics had grown so partisan in recent years that I found it refreshing to hear someone say we had to move beyond that. Bush had been able to do that in Texas, and he thought he could do it in Washington. If he did win this election, I certainly hoped he could bring people together.

As he left the New Hampshire studio he told me, "We're going to do better up here than people think."

He did not, of course. New Hampshire does not like to be taken for granted, and New Hampshire liked John McCain's straight talk. McCain beat Bush handily, and the loss put the Bush people into shock. They had been blindsided. From that day on, the Bush campaign turned right and took on a harder edge. To demonstrate that he was the true conservative in the race, Bush went to South Carolina and appeared at Bob Jones University, a far-right fundamentalist institution that had once vilified his own father as being an agent of the devil.

I have always wondered if Bush's political strategists looked back on that *Face the Nation* interview in which Bush talked about reaching across party lines and building consensus and concluded that approach may have worked in Texas but would not work in a presidential campaign. Whatever the case, after that interview, Bush's emphasis seemed to shift from building consensus to finding ways to strengthen ties to his base, the conservative side of the Republican Party. The strategy worked. Bush had more money, and he went on to defeat McCain and win the presidency.

*Face the Nation* and the other Sunday shows had become major battlegrounds in presidential politics and the trend would continue. As 2004 dawned, all of the major Democratic candidates who were competing to oppose George Bush had appeared on *Face the Nation* and the other Sunday broadcasts numerous times. For the candidates of Campaign 2004, no stop on the campaign trail would be more important or attract more attention that when they appeared on one of the Sunday morning talk shows.

The Sunday primaries had become part of the political landscape.

10

---

# The Longest Story

## The Saga of Clinton vs. Starr

*I know, I know, what she did was wrong. But I felt sorry for the kid.*

The author in a weak moment, September 1998

Our normal practice at *Face the Nation* is to stay as close to the news as we possibly can. Our objective each week is to land an interview with the key player in whatever happens to be the top story of the moment. Only on Thanksgiving weekend do we make an exception. Then we step back from the spot news and invite a panel of historians to take a longer view. Over the years, we have had scholars ranging from David McCullough and Robert Dallek to presidential historian Alan Lichtman and Theodore Roosevelt's biographer, Edmund Morris. Bill Clinton's biographer, David Maraniss, has also appeared frequently on our Thanksgiving shows.

In truth, we were driven by necessity, rather than noble motives, when we began the historian shows. It is all but impossible to book public officials on Thanksgiving weekend. It is one of two weekends (Christmas is the other) when even the lure of live television does not override most people's desire to be with family and friends. In any case, the historian shows have proven to be popular with our viewers, and especially with journalists, who have told me over the

*Democratic Congressman Barney Frank and Republican Congressman Asa Hutchinson had little to say to each other as they waited to be interviewed during the impeachment battle. (Karin Cooper–Polaris Images for CBS)*

years they enjoy hearing someone other than reporters and officials involved in the daily news grind. (Yes, even the talking heads sometimes tire of the same old talking heads!)

As the panel of historians gathered in the *Face the Nation* studio on Thanksgiving weekend 1997, the midterm elections were looming. Bill Clinton was nearly two years into his second term, and I asked historian Doris Kearns Goodwin a question about what she thought Clinton's legacy would be.

She smiled and said, "Maybe something to do with a balanced budget," and then added, "I suppose it depends on what happens in these next couple of years."

If only we had known what those "next couple of years" would bring. Clinton had been dogged by one kind of investigation or another almost from the moment he had come to office. But the chaos of those years would be nothing compared to those "couple of years" to come. We had already heard about a questionable land deal called "Whitewater" that had taken place back in Arkansas while Clinton was governor and about a woman named Paula Jones who claimed he had sexually harassed her during that time. But in those "couple of years" to come, we would be introduced to Monica Lewinsky and as bizarre a cast of characters as has ever trod the Washington stage.

Over the next year and a half, we would learn of the president's Oval Office trysts with the 24-year-old intern. We would hear accusations that the president had lied about it when he gave a sworn deposition to a lawyer for Paula Jones, questions that eventually led to impeachment proceedings in the Congress. When the leaks about the young intern surfaced in January, it set off a mad chase among reporters to interview her.

Her lawyer, a hitherto obscure California attorney named William Ginsburg, became the toast of New York and Washington. America's top journalists fawned over him and wined and dined him in the best restaurants, all in an effort to get the first interview with Lewinsky, whose chief job at the White House had been ordering pizzas during late-night work sessions.

Over the next 15 months, from January 1998 until February 21, 1999, we gave more attention to the scandal than any story since the Vietnam War. Over those 54 weeks, we carried reports about the scandal on 49 broadcasts. On most of those broadcasts, we devoted the entire program to it.

When I revealed those statistics during a broadcast in 2003, many viewers wrote to complain. They argued no story was worth the attention we had devoted to that one. I disagree. There was no joy in covering this story, and as it always is when a story involves sex, no one—including the press—came away from it looking better. As I wrote in my book, *This Just In: What I Couldn't Tell You on TV*, there were no heroes in this story—not among the president and his defenders, not among Ken Starr and those who pursued him and not among those of us who covered it.

But it was a story that had to be covered. The president of the United States had been accused of lying under oath, and a majority of the House of Representatives had recommended that the results of a presidential election be overturned and the person who received 49 percent of the popular vote be removed from office.

The story of Monica Lewinsky was a familiar tale of office romance. A younger woman falls for an older and powerful man. Such stories usually end sadly and people are hurt, but the story is usually of consequence only to those involved. But this was not just any office; it was the Oval Office, as much a symbol of America as the Washington Monument. As tawdry as it was, it presented a challenge to those of us covering it. The question we had to answer was, Does this really matter? Having an affair may be a sin, but it is not against the law.

The usual rule in journalism is that a public official's private life is out of bounds unless he or she is doing something in private that has an impact on public responsibilities, or if a reporter uncovers information that a public official is not what he says he is. For example, an official who keeps a mistress on the side but claims to be a family man and uses his upright image to get elected is considered fair game. In politics, hypocrisy can be the equivalent of a felony, and in Washington, the cover-up can be worse than the crime.

In this case, an affair being carried on within the confines of the Oval Office was so reckless that it raised questions about the president's judgment, set off alarms about national security and raised the possibility the president could be blackmailed. It opened to suspicion every action the president took.

It was during the Clinton presidency that we were coming to know about Osama bin Laden and the threat he posed to America. When President Clinton launched cruise missile attacks on what was thought to be bin Laden's terrorist training headquarters in Afghanistan and what was believed to be a chemical weapons plant in the Sudan, questions arose about whether the missiles had been fired to draw attention from the president's problems with Monica Lewinsky.

I remember one Sunday when I asked General Hugh Shelton, the highly decorated chairman of the Joint Chiefs of Staff, if "you are convinced in your heart that this attack was a military action done for military reasons and did not have anything to do with Monica Lewinsky." His answer from the transcript:

SHELTON: I am convinced beyond the shadow of a doubt. The president throughout this looked at what options were available, not only military but other options and was very concerned about the actions that would be taken. He was very engaged through this period of time.

It was an unusual question to pose at the moment of a U.S. attack on two foreign countries, but it was a question that was being raised in Congress and a question being talked about all over the country. It was a period when Americans were just coming to hear about Osama bin Laden. As the years have passed, I have sometimes wondered if we would have paid more attention to the threat he posed had we not been distracted by Monica Lewinsky.

As for covering the story, the question for me was never whether we should devote so much attention to it, but *how* we went about it. I thought we did a good job on that. Producer Carin Pratt and I made a decision early on that we would cover the scandal as we would any other major story. We would try to give both sides, but we would not pair partisans on opposite sides just to hear them scream at each other. We also tried to give the story context from time to time by putting on "wise formers," such as one-time presidential candidate and senator Bob Dole, former White House staff chiefs such as Leon Panetta and Howard Baker, legal experts such as Robert Bork and media observers such as Stephen Brill. The idea was to hear from those who knew Washington well but were not directly involved in the controversy.

To be sure, we gave White House spokesmen such as Rahm Emanuel and Paul Begala their innings, just as we gave equal time to

*When Senator Orrin Hatch was late to the broadcast and I spotted him slumping in his car outside the studio, I thought he had suffered a stroke, but he turned out to be talking to the president on a cell phone and had lost track of time. (Karin Cooper–Polaris Images for CBS)*

their opposite numbers from the congressional Republican ranks. And like our competitors, we put on Monica Lewinsky's lawyer, William Ginsburg, hoping that he would give us the first exclusive interview with his client. (It didn't work.) But, in general, we left the minor characters to the cable channels.

It was on *Face the Nation* that one of the "formers," the man who had run against Clinton in the previous election, Bob Dole, offered what I thought was the best way to resolve the controversy.

After the House voted two articles of impeachment against the president—one saying Clinton had obstructed justice and the other charging that he had not told the truth—Dole came on *Face the Nation* with a plan to censure the president but not remove him from office. Under the Dole plan, the two articles of impeachment would be placed in a joint resolution to be voted on by both houses of Congress. The wording of Dole's resolution:

> *The Congress finds the President did not tell the truth, Congress finds that the President obstructed justice and then he [Clinton] signs that [document] in a public ceremony which would acknowledge, in effect, that he lied.*

Two of my favorite stories during that unpleasant 15 months had little to do with the substance of the story or its final outcome.

The first story had to do with the chairman of the Senate Judiciary Committee and how I mistakenly believed we had somehow "lost" him on a Sunday when he was supposed to appear on the broadcast as our lead guest. As it grew closer and closer to 10:30 A.M. when the broadcast airs live to our stations around the country, Orrin Hatch was nowhere to be found.

Hatch is one of the most reliable and decent men in Washington and a veteran of the Sunday talk shows, and when he had not shown by 10:20, I feared the worst.

Finally, I went outside our studio to look for him myself. And there, in the entrance to the CBS parking lot, was Hatch's SUV. I could see him slumped over in the seat and my first thought was he had suffered a heart attack or a stroke.

I ran to the car and beat on the windows and shouted, "Senator, are you all right?"

Hatch looked up sheepishly. He had not suffered a stroke. He was slumped over because he was talking on a cell phone.

"Senator," I pleaded, "get out of there. We're about to go on the air."

Hatch got out of car and apologized, saying he was sorry, but the president had called him just as he was turning into the parking lot.

Hatch said the President had called to ask his advice about how to handle the controversy and he felt he had to talk to him.

"I told him . . . ," Hatch said. For the first time in my life I

*Monica Lewinsky's lawyer, William Ginsburg, became such a media darling that one weekend he appeared on all five Sunday talk shows, a feat that became known as a "full Ginsburg."*

stopped someone who was trying to tell me what he had just told the president.

"Hold it for the broadcast," I instructed him as we hustled into the studio. We made it with a minute or so to spare, and once the broadcast began, what Hatch told the president ("forget the legal hairsplitting and tell the American people what happened") made a nice little nugget for the interview.

The other story that I'll never forget occurred the day that we invited Bob Bennett, the president's lawyer in the Paula Jones lawsuit, to be our guest. Gloria Borger was our guest questioner that day, and she brought up a report making the rounds that Jones claimed to know certain distinguishing characteristics about the president that would be known only to someone who had been intimate with him.

Bennett took the question head-on.

"The President," he declared, "is normal in size, shape and direction."

Gloria was stunned.

"I just hope my mother wasn't watching," she said later.

I asked Bennett after the broadcast how he knew such information, and he said he got it from the president's doctor, not from personal observation. When I asked if he thought the president would approve of what he had said, he laughed and said, "No, he's probably upset that I didn't say it was one of the biggest ones I ever saw."

I never felt that Clinton should be removed from office. To me, that is the most severe penalty allowed under our Constitution and one that should be reserved for traitors and those who sell out the country. Clinton was neither. I did believe he should have been censured or given some other penalty, the course favored by Dole and former President Gerald Ford. That was not the mind-set of conservative House Republicans. Even as polls showed a majority of Americans were against removing him from office and even after it became clear that Republican leaders in the Senate could not muster the votes needed to remove him, the House Republicans refused to consider censure and insisted on pressing for the ultimate penalty:

*President Clinton's lawyer, Bob Bennett, assured viewers the president's anatomy was "normal" in every way, one of the more surprising revelations in the broadcast's history.*

removal from office. Eventually, that allowed Clinton to walk away with no penalty.

After the impeachment battle passed, we assembled another panel of historians for our Thanksgiving weekend show of 1999. They had a far different view of Clinton's legacy from the panel of the year before when Doris Kearns Goodwin had said Clinton's legacy would depend on "the next couple of years."

To Clinton biographer David Maraniss, who appeared on the 1999 broadcast, there was a familiar pattern in the events of the previous months.

*MARANISS: It's an eerie pattern in his life. Branch Rickey [the late baseball executive] said that luck is the residue of design and with Bill Clinton, it's his design to just sort of play it out until the opponents overplay their hand. It happened in Arkansas many times. It happened in 1992 when he kept hanging in there during the campaign. In '94 after Gingrich took over, he let the Republicans overplay their hand and shut down the government. And he did it again this year with the Republicans.*

The panel did not believe that years from now, Clinton would be remembered as a major figure of his time, nor did Maraniss believe Clinton had shaped his era in any significant way.

*MARANISS: I don't think he will be remembered as having shaped the culture but I think he is almost a reflection of the modern American celebrity culture, for better or worse. I think many of the contradictions that you see in Bill Clinton, you see in the culture now, between ambition, idealism and wanting to take the easy road.*

If that is history's judgment, then it will be wrong to say that Clinton went unpunished.

Afterthought: Whatever history's judgment of Clinton, there is little question that those 15 months reflected the changes that have come to America in the age of instant communication: the 24-hour news cycle and the never-ending task of feeding the beast—finding enough news to meet the never-ending deadlines; the arrival of the Internet as the nation's national water cooler, a place where information—sometimes true and sometimes false—is passed on instantly and the era when Andy Warhol's prediction that eventually everyone will become famous for 15 minutes may have been fulfilled. I thought of Warhol's prediction when I read an offbeat story in the *New York Times* that caused me to pose the following question in my Sunday commentary.

### *Whatever Happened to That Lawyer, What's His Name?*

*When the Indonesian people finally dumped Suharto, the dictator who had bled the country for millions of dollars during 32 years of iron-fisted rule, it came as a shock to the old despot.*

*He apparently thought his people loved him. Wrong. To the sur-*

139

*prise of no one else, once he stopped handing out favors, the people who had been hanging around his headquarters disappeared.*

*There was a little story in the papers the other day about how blue he is because no one comes to see him anymore.*

*Even his guards no longer salute and only his pet parrot still calls him "Mr. President."*

*In fact, every time the parrot sees him, it screeches, "Good morning, Mr. President," which must get pretty old since it's a reminder that he isn't "Mr. President" anymore.*

*Well, call me sentimental but it got me thinking about Monica Lewinsky's old lawyer, William Ginsburg, and how he used to be the toast of programs like this one and how we all used to call him twice a day, in hope of landing an interview with his star client and then one day she wasn't his client.*

*Do you suppose that Barbara Walters and Mike Wallace still call? Sort of sad. I wonder if Ginsburg has a parrot to remind him of the old days.*

*If he doesn't I'll bet I know where he can get one—if Suharto hasn't strangled it already.*

# 11

---

# War at Home and Abroad

## 9/11, Anthrax and the Terrorists

*My message to the terrorists is you don't know what you have gotten yourselves into.*

Secretary of State Colin Powell, September 23, 2001

The attacks on September 11, 2001, were the worst thing that have happened to America since World War II, and it was the hardest story that any of us at CBS News had ever covered because it was not a story about others; it was a story about us as well. Reporters are used to covering other people's tragedies. We don't enjoy it, but it is part of what we do, and we learn to do it under the worst of circumstances. But on 9/11, it was our families and friends who were at risk, our homeland that had come under attack.

In New York, every CBS News reporter, producer and photographer—without exception—who went to Ground Zero that day had a near-death experience. Some have not recovered completely from breathing the dust in the air that day. Some still have nightmares. In my book *This Just In*, I recounted how the youngest member of the *CBS Evening News* staff watched in horror as the second plane crashed into the tower where her wheelchair-bound father worked and how she never heard from him again; how Eric Shapiro who

*As the administration planned its response to the 9/11 attacks, Democratic Senator John Kerry and Defense Secretary Don Rumsfeld shared information while waiting to appear on* Face the Nation. *(Karin Cooper–Getty Images for CBS)*

directed the early coverage did so believing his own daughter had been killed in the attack.

In Washington, it was believed that the White House was the next target, and key White House personnel including the vice president were hustled into the bomb shelter below ground. Our team of White House correspondents—John Roberts, Bill Plante, Mark Knoller and Peter Maier—were told to evacuate the White House immediately. Maier managed to broadcast a report on what was happening from a nearby office building.

CBS producers inside the U.S. Capitol fled from the building, believing it under attack. I had been in traffic at the foot of Capitol Hill when our bureau chief, Janet Leissner, told me to turn away because there were reports another plane was headed to the Capitol. We later learned that the plane was forced down by the passengers in Pennsylvania. We set up a camera across the street from the White House on the roof of the Chamber of Commerce building, and I spent most of the day there. It would be the beginning of the longest continuous coverage in the history of CBS News. We had begun broadcasting when the first plane crashed into the first tower on Tuesday morning and we did not stop for the next 93 hours and 5 minutes, when we finally signed off at 6:00 A.M. Saturday morning. An hour later, we would be back on the air with the regularly scheduled *CBS Saturday Morning News*.

At *Face the Nation*, we asked our news chief, Andrew Heyward, to give us more time so we could do an hour-long broadcast on Sunday.

*On the Sunday after 9/11, correspondent Byron Pitts described rescue efforts under way at Ground Zero.*

He said "no problem" and asked, "Could you do a two-hour show?" Of course, we said yes.

We were all exhausted, but we spent Saturday planning what I thought turned out to be one of our finest broadcasts. Our mission has always been to tell viewers as much as we can about a story and then put it in context, and I felt we were able to do that under very difficult circumstances. Every key official connected to this story with the exception of the president was on *Face the Nation* that day.

Our lead guest was the secretary of state, Colin Powell, and he told us we were facing a new kind of enemy that had completely misread America. From the transcript:

*The gravity of what had happened could be seen on the faces of Senators Richard Shelby and Chuck Hagel as they waited to be interviewed. (Karin Cooper–Polaris Images for CBS)*

*POWELL: My message to the terrorists is you don't know what you have gotten yourselves into. You have pulled America together in a time of tragedy. You will now see what we are made of. You'll see the steel that holds this country together. You'll see our determination, you'll see our firmness and you will realize you are at war with a powerful adversary who will defeat you and we will do what is necessary.*

More interesting in retrospect was Powell's answer when Gloria Borger noted that Saddam Hussein had boasted that "the American cowboy is reaping the fruits of his crimes of humanity." She asked Powell if he thought Saddam Hussein had any connection to the attack. From the transcript:

*Colin Powell never loses his cool during an interview, but that Sunday even he appeared a little jarred by the events of the week. (Karin Cooper–Polaris Images for CBS)*

POWELL: *This is an irrelevant individual sitting there with a broken regime. He pursues weapons of mass destruction. He is the greatest threat in that region because he refuses to abide by the simplest standards of civilized behavior. So we'll continue to contain Saddam Hussein, we will keep his regime under sanctions and we will do what is necessary when it becomes necessary when we choose to.*

BORGER: *But are there any of his fingerprints on this particular attack?*

POWELL: *At the moment we see no fingerprints between Iraq and what happened last Tuesday. But we are looking. We'll pull it up by its roots, we will find out who is responsible and we will determine what connections exist between various regimes around the world who participate in this kind of thing.*

Later in the broadcast, we got reaction from New York Senators Chuck Schumer and Hillary Rodham Clinton; perspective from three key senators, Joe Biden, Chuck Hagel and Richard Shelby; and analysis from former Secretary of Defense William Cohen, former Air Force Chief of Staff Ronald Fogelman, terror and germ war expert Judith Miller of the *New York Times* and stock market expert Ed Yardeni of Deutsche Bank.

I felt then and still feel that America came away from 9/11 a stronger country, and I closed the broadcast that day with this commentary:

> *Americans came together this week as they have not come together since World War II.*
>
> *You could see it and feel it and not just in the calls for retaliation.*
>
> *I noticed it first, as I was driving to the Capitol last week.*
>
> *The road rage of rush hour evaporated like a morning dew.*
>
> *Instead, flags flew from car phone antennas and drivers waved and gave a thumbs-up when you signaled to change lanes.*
>
> *You could feel it at the Capitol. Congress passed a $40 billion emergency aid bill and passed it with an unprecedented unanimous vote.*
>
> *But that was only part of it.*
>
> *When Republican leader Trent Lott and his Democratic counter-*

*part, Tom Daschle, approached the microphones to announce it, Lott had his arm around his old political foe.*

*Someone said that America changed forever last week, but that is not quite right. Because I am old enough to remember an America that used to be this way.*

*That is the easy part for us to forget, because we got off track in the '60s.*

*A great cynicism gripped the country after the death of John Kennedy and as we became bogged down in Vietnam, a war we never understood, we lost faith in government, our institutions and each other.*

*But on Tuesday, we somehow remembered how it used to be and how we used to be. We understood that we are all in this together, that any one of us could have been on one of those planes, that our children or brothers could have been in one of those buildings and that it could happen again.*

*Many things happened on Tuesday, and I think one of them may be that we have finally gotten past Vietnam.*

*Those who wanted to get America's attention got it, and they will rue the day they did.*

Before 9/11, we had come to confuse heroes with celebrities, but 9/11 got us back on track. Once again, the heroes of my youth—firefighters, police, soldiers, other people who risk their lives to save others—are America's heroes.

During Vietnam, Americans became so disillusioned with the war that they turned on the soldiers who had been sent off to fight the war—soldiers who many times had been draftees who had hated the war as much as those who opposed it back home. After 9/11, we would not make that mistake.

As we left the studio that afternoon, our producer, Carin Pratt, said, "If there is a part of this story we didn't cover, I don't know what it was."

The next Sunday, one of our guests, Connecticut Senator Joe Lieberman, unveiled the details of a proposal to create a department of homeland security, an umbrella agency to bring all the terrorist fighting arms of the government from the Coast Guard to the Secret Service under one overall head.

Democrats controlled the Senate at that point, and Lieberman eventually got his committee to approve the concept on a straight party line vote. All the Democrats voted for it, all the Republicans against it. The White House also came down hard in opposition to the idea.

Later, of course, President Bush would reverse course and adopt the concept as his own, and he would successfully push Congress to approve the plan.

Lieberman later told me (off camera) that a Republican senator on his committee who had opposed the idea asked in jest, "I know why I was against this. Explain to me why I am now going to vote for it [which he did]."

America was still in shock in those first weeks after 9/11, and what we did not understand was that the story was only going to get worse.

Just as we were beginning to believe the story was shifting from the homeland to Afghanistan, where U.S. Special Forces were trying to find Osama bin Laden, we were blindsided by another blow on the domestic front: anthrax.

On October 5, less than a month after the 9/11 attacks, a Florida man died of anthrax inhalation, and health officials began an investigation into whether there was some connection to a bioterrorism attack. A week later at NBC, Tom Brokaw's assistant was diagnosed with anthrax after opening a letter addressed to Brokaw. Anthrax letters were also received at ABC and CBS, and three days later, on October 15, a letter addressed to Senate majority leader Tom Daschle was also found to contain anthrax. The Hart Senate Office Building, which contained offices for more than 50 U.S. senators, was closed, and Daschle's employees, some of whom were pregnant, were put on a powerful medicine called ciprofloxacin. Those of us who covered the Senate and had been in the Hart Building were also told to take it as a precaution. The drug can have powerful side effects, and I had begun taking it on the Friday before I interviewed Secretary of State Powell on *Face the Nation*. During the interview, I asked Powell a question, and as he answered, I completely lost my train of thought and for a moment became totally disoriented. I regained my composure as quickly as I had lost it, and it didn't show on the air. Doctors told me that sometimes happens when taking this drug.

On October 17, the Capitol was thrown into complete pandemonium when traces of suspected anthrax were found in office buildings of the House of Representatives. House leaders shut down operations until all the buildings could be declared safe from anthrax. New complications arose when more anthrax was found in a postal facility where congressional mail is received. Tragically, some postal workers died.

*National Security Adviser Condoleezza Rice in a quiet moment before going on camera. (Karin Cooper–Polaris Images for CBS)*

Who sent the anthrax letters has never been determined, and whether it was the work of terrorists or a lone madman remains unknown. It was one more blow to a capital city that had not yet recovered from the 9/11 attacks.

Again at CBS News, we found ourselves covering another story that involved us. Again, we were working around the clock. For those of us in Washington, there was the added anxiety of not knowing where the next anthrax attack might come or how powerful it could be, but we knew this was nothing to be taken lightly. One day Tennessee Senator Bill Frist, who is also a medical doctor, told me that had the amount of anthrax that been contained in the letter to Senator Daschle gotten into the air-conditioning system of the Hart Office Building where it had been found, it would have killed everyone in the building had it gone untreated. It was not the sort of thing that those of us who worked in the building felt comfortable about as we entered the Capitol each day.

At first, Senate leaders expected to have the Hart Building reopened in a matter of days, but as the cleaning process took longer and longer, the building would not reopen until January 2002. Senate staffers (who called themselves "Hart transplants") camped out in government buildings throughout Washington, and senators shared tiny offices within the Capitol building, often with no phones connecting them to staffers.

When Frist appeared on *Face the Nation* the following Sunday, he confirmed what was becoming clear: if there was a biological attack on America, we were unprepared to handle it. On anthrax for example, from the transcript:

FRIST: *The problem would be that if that occurred all over the country, or if an airplane flew over and exposed hundreds of thousands of people, you couldn't handle them at our public health infrastructure, you couldn't handle them at the local emergency room. We have to build up that public health infrastructure. . . . We're much better prepared than we were a year ago; five years ago we were not prepared at all.*

But it was not anthrax that Frist saw as the real danger. The real danger, he said, was if a terrorist unleashed a smallpox attack, which, he said, would be easier to do and deadlier. Again from the transcript:

*FRIST: Smallpox has huge consequences, much more than an atomic bomb, if it were released. Why? Because unlike anthrax, it's contagious. There was an exercise called Dark Winter—a plan for preparedness. And we know by introduction—on that model—in three different states that within three months it spread to 25 states, spread overseas—there are no boundaries there. About 2 million people would be dead, 5 million people sick at the end of three months. That makes it alarmist. The good news is that smallpox has been eradicated from the face of the earth, The flip side of that is we know there is some smallpox in this country, in Russia and possibly other countries.*

It was disquieting news to say the least. But it was news the American people needed to know. As the weeks became months, Senators and their staffers finally got back into their offices. The Hart Building—after spending more than $23 million clearing it of anthrax germs—was finally declared safe and no lives were lost. Postal workers were not so lucky. Two died after coming into contact with anthrax-laced mail meant for Capitol Hill.

Satellite technology was becoming so good that as the months rolled by, we often went directly to Afghanistan for on-the-scene reports from our correspondents there. Sunday after Sunday, Alan Pizzey, the workhorse of the CBS News foreign staff, would report the latest developments directly from the battlefield on the hunt for Osama bin Laden.

Through the fall, we continued to concentrate on the possibility of a biological attack on America and the drive to topple the Taliban in Afghanistan. U.S. officials continued to say they believed bin Laden was behind the attacks and that he was hiding somewhere in the mountains of Afghanistan. A connection with Saddam Hussein was not yet being talked about, but already the administration

*After the Capitol and the White House were evacuated on the day of the attack, I spent the rest of the day reporting from a rooftop adjacent to the White House. Smoke from the burning Pentagon can be seen over my left shoulder.*

was hearing from those who thought the hunt for bin Laden was not going fast enough.

On November 4, I closed off the broadcast with this commentary. From the transcript:

*SCHIEFFER: When people asked, "Are we winning this war?" I thought back to Vietnam when people asked that a lot. What it took us a while to understand back then was that when we have to ask, we are not winning.*

*Winning is apparent. We'll know we're winning when Osama bin Laden is dead or behind bars and those people in the caves come out with their hands up and when we can open a letter without wondering if it's going to kill us.*

*No, we are not winning, not yet anyway. Nor is this some adult version of "Are we there yet" and the government shouldn't try to treat it that way by pacifying us with soothing syrup. We don't need to keep hearing that everyone in the government has done everything right. What we need to know is that people are doing the best they can and those who were not have been moved out and that whatever the cost, we'll hang in there until things go our way and they will.*

*This country is just too big, too strong, too resourceful and has always shown too much resolve for it to come out otherwise.*

*They say the president is pondering what to tell the country this week. How about a little of that? And then a realistic assessment of just how hard this is going to be. Remind us, too, that this isn't Vietnam or about trying to help someone else.*

*It is about an attack on us that left thousands of our people dead.*

*If we keep that fact forever in mind, we'll eventually find a way to get this done.*

We were coming to understand just how difficult "getting this done" was going to be. On October 21, our Pentagon correspondent, David Martin, reported that on the first night of the war, one of the CIA's flying reconnaissance drone aircraft had located Mullah Omar, bin Laden's top official and strategist. But because he was next to a mosque, the Army commander, Tommy Franks, decided not fire on him for fear the mosque would be damaged. Franks had reportedly made the decision not to fire after checking with his legal adviser.

To me, the most interesting thing about rereading the transcripts three years later is how seldom the name of Saddam Hussein came up. In time, of course, he would become the main target in the war on terror, but from September 16, the first broadcast after 9/11, until the end of the year, Saddam Hussein and the threat he posed to America would be mentioned fewer than a half-dozen times and by only three officials: Secretary of State Colin Powell, Secretary of Defense Donald Rumsfeld and his deputy, Paul Wolfowitz. In each case, they mentioned him only in answer to questions posed by me or Gloria Borger.

# TIME LINE OF TERROR

September 11, 2001

8:46 A.M. American Airlines Flight 11 with 92 people on board crashes into the north tower of the World Trade Center.

9:03 A.M. United Airlines Flight 175 with 65 people on board crashes into the south tower of the World Trade Center.

9:40 A.M. American Airlines Flight 77 with 64 people on board crashes into the Pentagon.

9:48 A.M. The U.S. Capitol and the White House are evacuated after reports of another plane headed to Washington.

9:59 A.M. The south tower of the World Trade Center collapses.

10:10 A.M. Hijacked United Flight 93 with 44 on board is forced down and crashes in Pennsylvania as passengers resist hijackers.

10:28 A.M. The north tower of the World Trade Center collapses.

September 17

The stock market reopens and the Dow Jones Industrial Average drops 681 points, the largest point drop in history but only 7.1 percent of the market's total value.

September 21

In Afghanistan, the Taliban rejects U.S. demands to hand over Osama bin Laden as the U.S. military buildup begins.

October 5

A 63-year-old Florida man dies of anthrax.

October 15

The Hart Senate Office Building closes after Senate majority leader Tom Daschle receives letter containing anthrax.

October 17

Congress is thrown into pandemonium and the House of Representatives closes as House office buildings are searched for anthrax.

November 12

A commercial jetliner crashes in Queens, New York, killing 260
people. Terrorism is suspected but later rejected.

December 7

The Taliban surrenders the last stronghold in Afghanistan.

December 11

Zacharias Moussaoui is the first person indicted in connection
with the terrorist attacks.

December 22

Hamid Karzai, head of Afghanistan's interim government, is
sworn in.

American Airlines flight attendants and passengers subdue the
so-called shoe bomber, Richard Reid, on a flight from Paris
to Miami.

———

# The War in Iraq

## Combat Coverage in Real Time

*Is there a good reason to go to war? Have we engaged all instruments of national power in search of a peaceful solution? Have we set forth clear goals? Does the objective merit risking American lives? . . . Have we been honest with ourselves and with the world about the risks of action, but also about the less obvious risks of inaction?*

Questions Defense Secretary Donald Rumsfeld asked
himself as America prepared for war in Iraq in 2003

Vietnam became known as the living room war as night after night, television brought the war home to Americans in a personal way they had never known before. But those pictures were usually two days old, recorded by cameras that used film, which had to be shipped by aircraft back to the United States.

During the Gulf War, technology had advanced to the point that for the first time, we heard live reports from CNN correspondents in Baghdad as the enemy capital came under aerial bombardment.

When the Iraq war began in early 2003, the technology had become so sophisticated that CBS News correspondents were not only in Baghdad as it was being attacked by U.S. bombers, they were

*We cut our interview short with correspondent John Roberts after Marines told him to dig a foxhole because enemy forces were in the area.*

also reporting live from specially equipped television stations on wheels that accompanied American ground troops as they made their way toward the Iraqi capital. Equipped with video phones and tiny satellite dishes, they were able to broadcast even during hair-raising nighttime rides through choking Iraqi dust at speeds of up to 40 miles per hour.

"We knew going in that the technology would make Iraq a watershed for war coverage," said CBS News president Andrew Heyward.

Throughout the Iraqi war, there were few Sundays at *Face the Nation* when we did not talk live to one of our correspondents in the field. The reports became so routine and the pictures so good that it was easy—even for those of us in television—to forget the constant danger that the reporters faced and the logistical and technological challenges they overcame.

To say the least, it was a lot harder than it looked. Just ask CBS

News White House correspondent John Roberts, the lead reporter for the CBS coverage of the war.

The reports that Roberts and the other CBS News people were able to beam back to the United States were the result of months of planning, training and, in many cases, the ability to overcome bad breaks in situations that were always dangerous.

Roberts's experiences on the road to Baghdad are testament to that. Months before the war began, he attended a special survival school for correspondents set up by the military. In December 2002, three months before the war began, CBS News executives got Pentagon permission to outfit a special vehicle that would allow Roberts and his crew to join one of the military convoys transporting ground troops into Iraq. Two producers in the London Bureau, Randy Joyce and Patrick Starling, began scouting for a vehicle that could be converted into a television station on wheels. They found just what they wanted in the showroom of an auto dealer in Dubai: a civilian version of the military's workhorse, the Humvee. They bought it on the spot. Over the next two months, they installed two video phones inside and two tracking antennas on the roof and hung five remotely controlled cameras—three inside, one on the front and one on the back. They also packed a stationary transmitter inside that could be used to beam pictures to satellites when the vehicle was stopped.

In a final touch, they painted it a military tan, and there began a nightmare tale. When they tried to get the vehicle with its fine new paint job into Kuwait, where the American forces were massing, Kuwaiti customs agents turned them back, saying that civilians could not bring a military vehicle into the country. The CBS men argued—to no avail—that it was *not* a military vehicle, just painted like one. When the Kuwaitis refused to budge, they drove back to their garage and repainted it in its original color. Sorry, the Kuwaitis responded, it is against the law to paint a military vehicle so that it looks like a civilian vehicle. After weeks of haggling, the customs agents finally relented, and Roberts's vehicle was allowed into Kuwait.

John was assigned to the Marines 2nd Light Armored Reconnaissance Unit, and when the unit moved out and headed toward Baghdad, John, Joyce, Starling and technician Kurt Spitzer wedged themselves into the vehicle and began one of the wildest car trips any of them had ever experienced.

"We drove at night in a huge convoy—hundreds of vehicles," Roberts remembered . . . the trucks and armored personnel carriers were about 50 feet apart, but the dust from the vehicle ahead was so thick you couldn't see its lights. And to make it worse we were wearing night-vision goggles, which are two-dimensional. It was like trying to drive while watching the road on a television screen; there was no depth perception at all."

As wild as it was, the vehicle's engine conked out a hundred miles into Iraq—unable to run on the only fuel available, the JP8 military mixture that is standard for Marine vehicles but not civilian cars.

*CBS executives feared the Army would block correspondent Mark Strassmann from reporting that an American enlisted man had tried to kill his officers, but the Army allowed the report to go through.*

The CBS team could never again get the engine running, and as a result they made the rest of the trip to Baghdad being towed by a Marine wrecker.

"It became the Disneyland Ride from Hell," Roberts said. "Here we were in this vehicle with a steering wheel and gears, but it was like a ride in an amusement park. We had no control whatsoever."

At several points they came under enemy fire.

"There was one stretch there where the fedayeen were on one side of the road, and to keep them pinned down, Marines on the other side of us would fire between our vehicles as we passed by.

"At one point we just stuck our cameras out the windows and tried not to think about the fact that we were in a civilian vehicle that had no armor on it like the Marine vehicles."

For all his troubles with the vehicle—during one stop, he took refuge under it while he talked by satellite phone to a mechanic in Ohio—Roberts still managed to file perceptive reports from the battlefield.

During the Gulf War, the military had kept correspondents well back from the action, but Roberts and his colleagues were never out of danger.

In the early days of the invasion, Roberts made contact with us on *Face the Nation* one Sunday morning, when his convoy made a brief stop. But his report had to be brief because once the convoy stopped, the Marines had given him a shovel and told him to dig a fighting hole: there were hostile forces in the area who might be tempted to fire on the stopped convoy.

We held follow-up questions to his report to a minimum so he could get to his digging.

Roberts and his team were part of a force of several hundred correspondents, photographers, producers and technicians that CBS News sent to the war zone after CBS News senior vice president Marcy McGinnis issued a call for volunteers on September 26, 2002. In her memo, McGinnis listed 12 cities where CBS teams might be based and rated them from "extremely" to "moderately" dangerous.

She said the company would furnish nuclear, biological and chemical suits plus flak jackets and body armor to all personnel assigned to the war zone.

McGinnis had directed the coverage in the wake of 9/11, and CBS News president Heyward had turned to her once more to direct what he knew would be a bigger and even more complicated assignment.

"Basically, we began planning for something that had never been done before," Heyward said, "covering a war live—in real time. This would not be Vietnam where the filmed battle scenes had to be shipped by air freight back to the United States. Nor would it be anything like the Gulf War when correspondents and cameras were kept so far away from the action that most of pictures that Americans saw had been shot by TV cameras on board the aircraft carrying laser-guided bombs. Tracking those bombs as they zeroed in on targets made for spectacular pictures in the beginning, but there were so few pictures of American ground troops that after awhile, the coverage began to look more like an electronic video game than a war."

Neither the military nor the news organizations had been pleased with the coverage of the Gulf War. The military had barred reporters from going into the areas where the action was taking place unless they were members of press pools organized by military public relations officers who accompanied the correspondents and photographers. Unfortunately, military commanders generally would not allow the press pools into combat areas until the fighting was over.

As preparations of the Iraq invasion moved forward, Defense Secretary Donald Rumsfeld and his top public affairs aide, Victoria Clarke, offered a new proposal to the media: the "embed" plan. If the civilian correspondents would agree not to report anything that might endanger the safety of a military unit, they would be assigned to travel wherever that unit went and free to report on its activities without fear of censorship.

"We understood that the military plan would give us unprecedented access," Heyward said. "But we had to think about two things before we decided to accept it—first, would we be giving up our independence, and second, would putting our reporters in such close, constant contact with the troops co-opt them? Could they be objective in reporting the story?

"We decided those were real concerns, and instead of saying those things could never happen, we decided they might and that we had to keep a constant watch on it.

"In the end, we decided to do it, but we made sure the military understood we would also be covering the story with reporters who were attached to no particular unit, and we made sure our viewers would be hearing from a variety of independent voices—retired generals whom we hired as consultants and especially David Martin, our terrific Pentagon correspondent, who would play a key role in the coverage."

Although some news organizations were leery about participating in the embed program, most of us at CBS News thought the plusses far outweighed the minuses and were enthusiastic about it.

But we had no illusions. We knew we could expect cooperation from the military as long as the news was good. The real test would come when the news turned bad, as inevitably it does in war. The test would come early, when correspondent Mark Strassmann and cameraman Don Lee were wakened one Saturday night by three explosions.

Strassmann and Lee had been embedded with the 101st Airborne, which was still on the Kuwaiti side of the border, but the blasts were so loud they knew they were close by. The newsmen assumed they were under attack by enemy mortars or artillery. Lee grabbed his camera and ran outside. The two quickly realized the blasts had come from hand grenades within the camp itself.

It was quickly determined that a disgruntled soldier who had been assigned to guard the ammunition dump had stolen grenades and tossed them into tents where the unit officers were sleeping. The attacks left one of the officers dead and several others wounded. Lee began to shoot pictures. Some of the troops tried to stop him, but when he explained that he was being careful not to show the faces of the wounded, he was allowed to continue.

The officers checked the unit personnel records and discovered that a soldier who was missing was a recent convert to Islam.

"This was the worst news of all," Lee said. "The realization that the bad guys were inside our camp wearing our uniforms."

The missing soldier was soon located hiding in a bunker and holding a grenade. One of the officers jumped into the bunker and disarmed him.

"The officers figured out that the man was mentally deranged and not part of an enemy plot," Lee said. "Because we were there and saw it all, we believed them, which to me, showed the value of the embed program. If reports had gotten out that the Iraqis had somehow infiltrated our own military forces, it could have been devastating for morale."

Lee, using a digital camera, was able to transmit the video he had shot back to CBS News headquarters within ten minutes using Strassmann's computer.

It would prove to be quite an evening for Lee and Strassmann. As things were getting back to normal in the camp after the grenade attack, Lee saw a bright light in the sky and instinctively shouldered his camera to photograph it.

"We thought it was one of our Patriot missiles knocking down one of the Iraqi Scud missiles," Lee said. "But we found out later it was the first serious accident of the war—the Patriot had mistakenly hit a British jet with two people on board."

The nightmarish evening had happened just a few hours before *Face the Nation* aired and Strassmann told the story to our viewers and showed Lee's pictures. From the transcript:

STRASSMANN: *There is a lot of disbelief and shock, and a sense of betrayal here. These guys always realize there could be a threat from outside the camp. Bob, I don't think anybody really suspected there could be a threat from inside the camp.*

And for the accidental downing of the British Tornado jet, this from the transcript:

*STRASSMANN: It was crazy. I mean right in the middle of this sneak attack on the tents here, we looked up in the sky and thought it was just a flare. Then somebody said, "Oh wait, that's a Patriot" and it looked like fireworks had gone off in the sky . . . then we heard it was a missile that had knocked down some sort of incoming Iraqi missile and then . . . that it inadvertently knocked down a British fighter coming back from a mission.*

It was the kind of gritty eyewitness reporting that could have come only from a reporter who had been there when it happened.

I had always favored the embed program, and for me that story alone proved its value. Heyward was in the New York control room that morning as the story was being fed in from Iraq, and he agreed. This was not good news, but the military officers allowed us to broadcast it.

"I knew then that we had made the right decision," Heyward said.

We had expanded *Face the Nation* from its usual 30 minutes to 1 hour that morning, and never have we better used our time.

*Scott Pelley reported live from behind a sand dune when U.S. Marines came under fire from a nearby village.*

At about the time Strassmann was dealing with the hand grenade attack, correspondent Scott Pelley and producer Bill Owens and their crew, who were not attached to any unit, had gotten in front of the main U.S. invading force. They had come upon a group of Marines guarding the Iraqi port of Umm Qasr. The surprised Marines told them the journalists could spend the night with their unit, and the next morning a band of Iraqi soldiers opened fire from positions on the edge of the port. Two Marine platoons ran to the top of a sand dune and mounted a counterattack with rifles, heavy machine guns and mortars. The firefight went on for more than five hours and provided some of the most dramatic pictures of the entire war.

When the battle was seen later that morning on *Face the Nation*, Pelley reported that the Iraqis had adopted an unexpected tactic. From the transcript:

*PELLEY: Many of the Iraqi soldiers have shed their uniforms and put on civilian clothes and blended into the neighborhoods, and in groups of two or three they are taking shots at the Marines moving through town.*

U.S. commanders had not expected that, but it would prove to be a tactic that the Iraqis used over and over. As the American invasion force drove on toward Baghdad, many Iraqi soldiers did not stand and fight but simply disappeared with their weapons into the civilian population.

The war in Iraq was as dangerous an assignment as any of our correspondents and camera crews had ever been given. Throughout the war and in the months afterward, we got the same kind of courageous reporting from Byron Pitts, Jim Axelrod, Alan Pizzey (who has probably been in more hot spots than any other CBS reporter alive), Lee Cowan, Lara Logan, Thalia Assuras, Kimberly Dozier, Elizabeth Palmer, Randall Pinkston, Mark Phillips, Richard Roth and Cynthia Bowers.

During the initial stages of the war, Bowers reported from an aircraft carrier where many of the bombing strikes were being launched, and Assuras had been embedded with the 4th Infantry Division.

Unfortunately for Assuras and Gabe Stix, the cameraman working with her, the unit was kept in reserve, and they sat out the early part of the war at Fort Hood, Texas. But there was still plenty of action left when Assuras finally got to Iraq in April.

"It was more like the Wild West than a war by the time I got there," she said later. "Baghdad was overrun by looters, there was no electricity and no police. It was chaos and the beginning of the sporadic attacks on the American forces who had tried to cordon off areas where the Americans were."

The Iraq war also saw more women assigned to combat coverage than any previous war. Lara Logan had reported from Baghdad during the initial bombing campaign, and in the months afterward, as troops fought an increasingly fierce guerrilla force, Elizabeth Palmer and Kimberly Dozier repeatedly took on dangerous assignments to report that story. Little has been written about the fact that they were women, a healthy sign, perhaps, of just how far women have come in their quest to be treated as equals.

At *Face the Nation*, we understood that our job was to go beyond the battlefield coverage, and so in the run-up to the war and after the initial combat, we brought on top officials Secretary of Defense Donald Rumsfeld, Secretary of State Colin Powell, Vice President Dick Cheney and senators from across the political spectrum who argued both for and against the war.

We also checked in regularly with CBS News Pentagon correspondent David Martin for context, analysis and late-breaking news. Martin is arguably the best-connected reporter in Washington who covers the national security beat—and maybe the most well-connected reporter covering any Washington beat.

Once, when the two of us were giving an informal briefing on how the media operate to an Army War College class, one of the colonels in the group asked how David checked information from his sources.

"A lot of the time," I told the colonel, "they check their information with him."

*Jim Axelrod was a real workhorse, filing report after report from the battlefield for* Face the Nation *and other CBS News broadcasts.*

I meant it. Whenever we brought Martin into the Sunday morning discussion on *Face the Nation,* I always felt he gave us an advantage over our competitors.

Several months into the campaign, I mentioned to Rumsfeld that I thought the embed program had not only given the American people a better understanding of the war; I thought it would also have a long-term impact on relations between the military and the media. Vietnam had left both institutions wary of the other, but based on my own experiences in Vietnam, I knew that reporters who were willing to go into the field and share the war with the soldiers soon earned the soldiers' respect. Equally important, I knew that such an experience caused the reporters to develop a new respect for and understanding of the military. I told Rumsfeld that our reporters in the field were telling me that the embed program was having just such an effect on both them and the soldiers fighting the war, and I thought the new understanding would pay positive dividends for years to come to both groups.

He agreed but admitted that neither he nor the military had really anticipated that in the beginning.

Rather, he told me, "Our goal when we decided to do this was to have American cameras and American reporters on the ground when we got to Baghdad. We knew the Iraqis would use every propaganda trick in the book to try and convince the world and their own people that Saddam Hussein's forces were turning back the American invasion.

"With American cameras there, we knew they couldn't lie and get away with it. The world would get the truth."

Ironically, more than a year later, when Dan Rather and a *60 Minutes II* crew broke the story of how American prison guards had abused Iraqi captives, it would be pictures taken by the American soldiers themselves that would tell the awful story of what had happened inside the prisons in Iraq.

On the Saturday afternoon after the story broke, we got a call from a White House official who said the nation's top military officer, General Richard Meyers, chairman of the Joint Chiefs of Staff, wanted to come on *Face the Nation* the next morning to talk about what had happened. Clearly the administration wanted Meyers to assure the American people that the military took the matter seriously and was determined to get to the bottom of it. We junked the broadcast we had planned to make room for Meyers, and he said what we had expected, that the situation was appalling, that the military was on the case and determined to see that justice was done. He said that once the military learned of it, "we took very quick action to investigate that situation." He said the investigation by another general had resulted in a report that ran in excess of 50 pages. Then, almost as an afterthought, he said he himself had not read the report.

That prompted the obvious question and I asked it, "Why would you not have seen the report?"

When Meyers replied that the report was still working its way up the chain of command, his answer was picked up by newspapers across the country. Columnists and editorial writers had the same question: If the military was serious about getting to the bottom of the problem, why had an investigation that had been completed two months earlier not yet made it to the desk of the military's top commander?

Nearly a month before the story aired, the *60 Minutes II* producers had notified the Pentagon that they were pursuing the story and asked for comment. The request was rebuffed, but over a three-week period Meyers twice asked Dan Rather to postpone the story. Rather and CBS agreed to both requests and did not broadcast the story until comments from a military spokesman were included in

*Correspondent John Roberts's mobile TV station. Unfortunately it broke down early in the war and was towed by Marine wrecker for most of the trip to Baghdad. (Randall Joyce for CBS News)*

170

the report. The disclosure that the military had been trying to keep the story off television and that top defense officials had not seen the results of their own investigation two months after its completion hit Capitol Hill like a thunderbolt.

Senators demanded to know why they had not been told of the episode and had learned about it only by seeing it on TV. There were demands for Rumfeld's resignation and the controversy over whether or not America should have gone to Iraq intensified. The words of CBS News president Andrew Heyward had been prescient: Iraq had been a watershed in war coverage. Television had allowed Americans to see war as they had not seen it before, and CBS News and *Face the Nation* had been pivotal in the coverage. Technology had been one reason, but only one. Ed Murrow once said of television: "This instrument can teach, it can illuminate, yes, it can even inspire, but it can do so only to the extent that humans are determined to use it to those ends. Otherwise it is merely wires and lights in a box."

If I had a wish, it would be that those words could be printed on every box containing a new piece of television equipment. The technology helped, but telling the story of the Iraq war came down to what it always does, the courage and dedication of reporters who are willing to go after the story and stick with it until they get it.

13

———

# Looking Ahead
## Television's Expanding Universe

*We should all be concerned about the future because we will have to*
*spend the rest of our lives there.*

Charles Kettering, "Seed for Thought," 1949

What will *Face the Nation* be like in years to come? I'm often asked
that question and my answer is, "Just the way it is as long as I have
anything to do with it." Let me tell why, and to do that, I want to
look back before I look forward.

It is hard to believe that a television program that began on
November 7, 1954, would still be around 50 years later, and it is
probably harder for me to believe than for you because I have worked
in television so long and know the industry's fickleness firsthand. But
to me, what is more remarkable than its longevity is that it has
remained basically the program its creator Frank Stanton envisioned
in the beginning: a live interview with one of the week's top newsmakers. Without exception over the years, whenever someone tried
to change it, disaster resulted and it was soon returned to its original
format.

While *Face the Nation* has remained the same, the world around
it has not. The broadcast debut came four years past the middle of

the twentieth century, a century in which the world underwent the most rapid and significant changes in its history. It was a century that can be more easily and neatly divided than most others. During its first half, enormous change came about because of two devastating wars and a great economic depression. Ancient empires fell, to be replaced by a new empire, the Soviet Union, and hundreds of independent states. By the year 2000, the Soviet Union too had collapsed, and America emerged as the world's only superpower, confirming what *Time* magazine founder Henry Luce had said at midcentury—that this was the American Century.

*Face the Nation* came to be almost exactly in the middle of this wondrous time, as the nations of the world were coming out of the great rearranging and were beginning to deal with the enormous change it had produced. The smashing of the Nazi empire had given the world new hope. Freedom begets the desire for more freedom. Great social movements began. Equally significant would be the explosion of technological advances.

In no other area would those technological advances have more impact than in communications as we developed the ability to move vast mountains of information instantly, from one point of the globe to another.

When *Face the Nation* first aired, broadcasting was in its early adolescence. In those days, most people still depended on print journalism—newspapers and magazines—as their primary source of news, and the news cycle had two deadlines. If a newsmaker said something in the morning, it wound up in the afternoon paper. If opponents wanted to respond, they generally did so that afternoon, which meant their statements appeared in the morning paper. In those days, people actually had time to think before they were required to speak.

In today's 24-hour news cycle, the world of cable television and the Internet, where Americans can choose from hundreds of television channels and thousands of web sites for news, there is a deadline every second. Instant communication—the ability to know about events as they are happening—has given us access to more information that any other peoples who have inhabited the earth at any other period of history. This new ability to know so much, and so quickly, has dramatically changed the way news is gathered and reported. Beyond that, it has had an enormous impact on nearly everything in our culture, from our government and religious institutions to the way we conduct business and raise our children. For the most part, these have been changes for the better. But there are downsides. The ability to know instantly about events has shortened our attention spans, made us more impatient and caused us to expect instant answers, which are seldom found.

For news outlets, the 24-hour news cycle has created a ravenous, unending appetite for information. "The beast must be fed," as we refer to it in the industry. The quest for something to put on the air never stops. Television can't show a blank screen when nothing is happening, so the drive to find information never ends. When new information can't be found, old information is repeated. When Howard Dean screams after losing a presidential primary, the scream is not only heard around the world, it is heard hundreds of times over the next 24 hours. Cable networks perform a valuable service: they deliver the news for the viewer who tunes in to find out what the big news is "right now." But if one listens for too long, it is possible to memorize the top stories as they are repeated over and over.

In a lecture on the impact of television that I delivered in 1981 at my alma mater, Texas Christian University, I observed that we are now witnesses to history, and the advantages are obvious. But I noted that wisdom does not necessarily increase at the same ratio that information becomes available, and when we are bombarded by momentous events, one result may be that we are only numbed by them.

In that lecture, I noted that television had not created the rush of modern times. Rather, it had only allowed us to see the events—the discord, the tragedies, the social movements—that were having an impact on our lives.

In the television age, there would be no secrets on the other side of the tracks, but as American society became more diverse and more complex, I said, it was also becoming more fractionalized, making it harder for its members to identify common goals. The one common thread that ran through our lives in this new world, I argued, was that we had all seen these momentous events on television. This fractionalized society, I said, would be fertile ground for single-issue politics—the politics that favors one pet issue to the exclusion of all others.

That lecture came long before the rise of cable, the Internet and the 24-hour news cycle, but what I predicted has come to be. What I did not understand was that as the news outlets multiplied, many would begin to cater to a specific portion of the population rather than the overall audience. In retrospect, that should not have surprised me. Magazines have always targeted specific audiences—sports magazines for people interested in sports, women's magazines for women and on and on. But magazines have never had the ability to reach so many people instantly.

The emphasis on catering to specific demographic groups by the new electronic media has led to "narrow"- rather than "broad"-casting. James Naughton, the former *New York Times* reporter, long-time managing editor of the *Philadelphia Inquirer* and recently retired president of the Poynter Journalism Institute, says this means television (and radio) are no longer the common experience for Americans that they once were.

"People no longer get the same information," he told me. "Each group finds the news that is tailored to its particular group."

I believe this is one reason the nation has become so polarized on so many issues and why—if my e-mail is any indicator—so many people now define objectivity as only that which agrees with their point of view.

Joel Kotkin, a senior fellow with the Davenport Institute for Public Policy at Pepperdine University, argued in the *Washington Post* that the polarization that grips America today is comparable to the situation in seventeenth-century England, when the royalist forces of Charles I and the Roundhead rebels led by Oliver Cromwell had such diverse views and hated each other so much that they could no longer share a common national vision. Cromwell and his group eventually overthrew the king and beheaded him. Kotkin foresees nothing like that in America's future, but he does pose a pertinent question: In the sharply divided politics of today, is anyone winning? He seems to believe the answer is no. And he points to signs that differences are widening rather than narrowing: Republicans and Democrats are becoming less likely to live next door to each other, attend the same church or subscribe to the same media.

Again, according to my e-mail, they are less likely to believe anything the other side has to say or even consider that an argument with which they disagree may have some merit.

Steven Luxenberg, the editor of *Outlook*, the *Washington Post* Sunday opinion section, says these suspicions have resulted in what he calls "the death of honest expertise."

He suggests that we tend to believe nothing unless we know the speaker or writer's motivation.

He began a March 28, 2004, essay with the words, "Before I offer a single thought, before I express a single opinion, I'll bet you're wondering: Who is this guy? What's his agenda? Where is he coming from?"

He is right, I am sorry to say. This sad state of affairs is the outgrowth of the mean spirit that now pervades our politics—the "I'm right, and if you wear a different political label you are wrong even before you say anything" attitude. But part of the blame must also go to television and what we have allowed to pass for political discourse on so many broadcasts—finding the person who takes the most extreme position on one side of an issue and pairing him or her with the person who holds the most extreme position on the other side and allowing them to scream at each other.

Wouldn't it be refreshing, during one of these "debates," if a person on one side made a statement and the person on the other side responded, "Well, there might be some merit to that . . ."? But it never happens. These matchups are designed to produce sparks and play gotcha! not to shed light on any particular issue.

As long as this format remains the norm, why shouldn't we, as Luxenberg asks, want to know if the person doing the talking is liberal or conservative, has a score to settle or is advancing his or her career? Or an even better question, is the person just a phony who will say anything to get on television?

That is why I believe there will always be a need for broadcasts such as *Face the Nation*. Sunday morning is the smartest morning on television—a time when serious ideas can be discussed at some length in serious ways. The discussions and the interviews that take place on *Face the Nation* and the other Sunday broadcasts are not like the talking-head shows of prime time. Sundays *are* different. Our job is to keep them so.

The great strength of America is that we have always been a nation that has benefited from the free and open discussion of all ideas, and for 50 years *Face the Nation* has been part of that process.

The great advances in human history have taken place not when doctrine took precedence over knowledge but when there was a climate favoring inquiry, but we must not mistake a sound bite contest for serious inquiry.

To those who will follow me, I offer these thoughts. Keep *Face the Nation* as it has always been, a place where ideas can be freely and fully explored. There are not many such places left. That was Frank Stanton's vision, and the need for such a program may be even greater in the future than it was when *Face the Nation* began. Understand as well the real strength of the medium at our command and its limits. The technology at our disposal is wondrous, but it is only a tool. The thoughts of the Greek philosophers were duplicated many times before there were even photocopying machines, the teachings of Moses and Christ and yes, Muhammad, spread around the world before there were satellites or even airplanes. It is the power of the message, the information that we transmit, that is the important part of what we do.

I have quoted Ed Murrow many times throughout this book, and I shall quote him once more because what he said many years ago remains true.

"Television can show us wondrous things," he said, "but we cannot yet take pictures of the most important thing—ideas, what goes on in the human mind."

Those of us who have been associated with *Face the Nation* are proud of what it has become. We recognize that its real power and influence come not from those of us who put the broadcast together each week but from the millions who have watched and listened over the years. Our job is to provide the information we believe you, as a citizen, need to know. You, in the end, decide what to do about it.

For that we thank you.

Telling the story of *Face the Nation* took a little longer than the stories we usually tackle, but it seems only natural to end this story as we always do because . . .

That's our broadcast. We'll see you next week on *Face the Nation*.

# Part II

# Behind the Scenes

———————

# My Thoughts Exactly

## The *Face the Nation* Commentaries

*Mine has been an unelected, unlicensed, uncodified office and func-
tion. The rules are self imposed. These were a few: Not to underesti-
mate the intelligence of the audience and not to overestimate its
information. To elucidate, when one can, more than to advocate. To
remember always that the public is only people, people only persons,
no two alike. To retain the courage of one's doubts as well as one's
convictions in this world of dangerously passionate certainties.*

The words of my teacher, Eric Sevareid, which
I have tried to follow in writing commentary.

The Sunday after Richard Nixon died in April 1994, we brought a
group of his former aides into the studio to talk about his legacy. As
we came to the end of the discussion, I thought it needed what those
of us in broadcasting call a "button," a few words summarizing what
had just been said. So as I came to the end of the program I said,
"Richard Nixon, who left the White House in disgrace but left this
life with some dignity."

I was stunned by the response. People wrote to thank me "for
putting the story into context," "for finding a pleasant way to end
the broadcast." Even self-professed Nixon haters wrote to say they

appreciated the way we had handled the story. I had thought little of it when I had expressed that opinion, but as the mail continued to roll in, I began to wonder about whether we should make a few closing thoughts about the news a regular feature. Producer Carin Pratt and I talked about it, and several weeks later I tried it again. Again, the response was overwhelmingly positive. No one had done commentary on CBS since Eric Sevareid had retired in 1977, and I wasn't sure if I was actually allowed to do it under the CBS News guidelines, but the response was so good that I continued to close the broadcast with a few personal thoughts when time allowed. I decided at one point to call our bosses in New York to see if commentary was allowed, but then I figured if it is not allowed, they'll call and tell me so. They didn't, and as the favorable comments continued to come in, I began to do commentary more and more often. By the end of the year, the commentaries had become a regular feature. Today, they generate more mail than any other part of the broadcast. It is virtually all e-mail now, and for the most part, it continues to be favorable, but as might be expected, as I have staked out positions on more and more issues, viewers often disagree and the critics' remarks are often scathing. The sharper tone reflects the growing use of e-mail. My theory is that in the past, viewers who had a complaint would sometimes write letters, and once they got the criticism out of their systems, they thought better of it and wadded up the first draft, threw it in the wastebasket or toned down their criticism before passing it on. No more. Now, they press the Send key, and we get the full, unvarnished benefit of their wrath. I get hundreds of e-mail messages a week—most of it about the commentaries. I try to read as much of it as I can, and unless it appears to be from a deranged person, I answer.

Often, those who have disagreed with the commentary respond and say they had no idea they would get an answer, nor did they expect I would read their letter personally. Scores of times, viewers have told me, they would not have made their criticism so personal had they known I read the mail myself. Whatever the case, I consider the commentaries a way to stay in touch with viewers and understand what is on their minds. From time to time, the questions they ask me become the questions I ask those who appear on the broadcast. I enjoy the dialogue with our viewers, and many of them seem to as well.

The hardest part of writing the commentaries is cutting them down to size. There is an old saying about the public speaker who rose to the podium and said, "I prepared a long speech today because I didn't have time to write a short one," and that is the great challenge of writing the commentaries. They generally run a minute and a half to two minutes—never more. That's about 400 words on paper. Because they are so short, they are more akin to constructing poems than essays. I have been told that my writing is spare, and it has to be. Television writing is like trying to stand up in a box that is not quite as tall as you are. There is never enough room to say all that you want to say. So it is with the commentaries. The first drafts are usually about twice as long as the finished product. People often ask me how many days in advance of Sunday morning I write them, and the answer is, "when I figure out what I want to write about." Sometimes it will come to me on Monday, but there have been many Saturday nights when I find myself struggling with what to say and how to say it. When the well runs dry, I usually turn to my wife, Pat, who will say something like, "Well, you've been ranting about such and such all week. Write about that."

I've always felt that politicians should write as many of their speeches as possible themselves, because writing a speech helps the writer to sort out his own thinking. The commentaries do that for me. For me, there is nothing like putting my thesis down on paper to see the fallacies of an argument. What sounds logical as I reason it out in my head may not seem so logical when I write it out. In this day when glibness counts for so much, I believe a lot of journalists and politicians would be better off if they wrote down what they believe before they said it aloud the first time. The one thing that bothered me as I began to write the commentaries was whether I was crossing the line that separates opinion journalism from straight reporting. Traditionally on newspapers, there is a division between the people who cover the news and those who work on the editorial page and comment on it. When I began to write the commentaries, I was still covering Congress full time (I no longer do) for the *Evening News*, which sometimes left me taking positions on Sunday on stories I had covered during the week. I decided I could do it because I do not promote any particular cause. Nor do I endorse political candidates. We also made sure that the commentaries are clearly labeled as such, and I have come to believe that the commentaries are actually a form of disclosure. If people know how I stand on an issue, it helps them to keep my reporting in context. My objective when I sit down each week to write a commentary has never been to convert someone to my way of thinking but merely to provoke thought, to explain a complicated subject or to call attention to a human foible that brings a smile, and in some cases to call attention to some noteworthy person who might have otherwise gone unnoticed.

The greatest compliment to me is not when viewers write to say they agree with my conclusion but when they say, "I really never thought of it that way before."

Here is a collection of the commentaries that have drawn the most reaction over the years, beginning with some thoughts on my favorite subject, politics.

## *Politics*

Politics has always been the beat that I loved most, the one to which I have devoted most of my professional life, but I have been saddened by what it has become. My commentaries on politics over the past ten years reflect my own disillusionment with the process, and as I sifted through them, it reinforced my conviction that we must find a way to get our system of selecting our leaders back on track. I begin this collection of commentaries with the essay I wrote on the eve of the presidential election of 2000 after I read that many of my own friends no longer voted.

## ON THE JOY OF VOTING

Several of my fairly famous colleagues have disclosed they no longer vote as a way of maintaining their neutrality as journalists. I admire their objective, but I don't understand their reasoning. Anyone who knows me knows how much I love my job, but it is a job. I wouldn't equate it with voting, which to me is my duty as a citizen, like paying the water bill.

I remember reading *The Rise and Fall of the Third Reich* as a young man and how surprised I was to learn the Nazis had used an election as a springboard to power. Had I lived in Germany then, I hope I could have voted against them. I wouldn't have wanted to be neutral on that one.

Besides, voting is just so much fun. As a reporter, I have to back up what I say with facts. But I need give no reason, marshal no argument for my vote. Maybe I just don't like the candidate's attitude. That's reason enough to vote against him. Or maybe I think a candidate really is qualified. Reason enough to vote for him.

It is my vote, and I can exercise it in any way I choose, but no candidate gets my vote unless I believe he or she deserves it.

We take voting so seriously at my house, my wife has instructed me never to tell even her who I vote for. She's afraid I'll disappoint her. Oh, ye of little faith! But isn't that the best part? We can tell everyone or no one.

So go vote. It's good for the country and good for you. Makes you feel big and strong.

*—November 5, 2000*

## HOW DID WE LET THIS HAPPEN?

When I was a little boy, my grandmother was certain that someday I would be president.

She was wrong, but that's how people used to think of the presidency, and the kind of dreams they used to have for their grandkids.

How different it is today.

When Colin Powell told us he did not want to go through the ordeal of running for president, most people nodded sympathetically and said they understood.

When it became known that his wife worried that he might be killed if he ran, most of us said, "Who can blame her?"

That is the most disturbing part. American politics has become so vile, the process of selecting a president so odious and dangerous, that good people in many cases just no longer want to be a part of it, and the rest of us have become resigned to it.

The next time you hear one of those sleazy ads on television and wonder what kind of impact it is having on our politics, just ask yourself this question: How long has it been since you've heard a grandparent say, "Someday I hope my grandson or granddaughter grows up to be president"?

—*September 26, 1999*


## DIRTY CAMPAIGNS


All last week, I was thinking, What if someone arrived from another planet and all he knew about our elections was what he learned from our campaign commercials?

First, the alien would conclude that only the dregs of our society run for office—the liars, thieves, adulterers and, yes, according to this year's commercials, the occasional murderer. If you go by the TV ads, decent people don't run for office.

I even saw one ad that accused a candidate of favoring public urination. Really.

The alien would also conclude that voter participation doesn't mean voting; it means using the phone a lot—as in, "Call so and so and tell him to stop lying or cheating or selling dope or whatever." How many times did we hear that one this year?

And by the way, if you don't travel much, you'll be interested to know those ads you hear on your hometown station are like McDonald's: go to the next town and they are just the same. Same accusations, same grainy photos, same raspy off-camera voice. Only the name of the person being attacked has been changed.

Campaign advertising has been dumbed down to the level of professional wrestling, the only difference being that wrestling is occasionally funny.

Are the ads effective? To me, they are more like cartoons, and I can't imagine anyone taking them seriously, but maybe some do. The candidates keep paying for them. And after all, some people believe wrestling is for real.

Here's the real shame of it. Some won and some lost, but there were some fine people running this year. But you would never know it from the campaign commercials.

—*November 10, 2002*


## CUSTOMER OF THE YEAR

After spending five years and at least $65 million of his own money, Steve Forbes folded his presidential campaign last week.

When he began his quest in 1995, there was some interest in his "flat tax" idea, but Americans have never looked on the presidency as an entry-level position—so the man who had never run for anything else never really caught on.

Who, then, kept telling him he could be president?

Anyone and everyone in the political community who had something to sell, be it polls or advice or commercials or whatever.

When you're the richest guy on the block, people line up to boost your ego.

I never doubted Forbes's sincerity or patriotism. But there are no short-cuts in American politics. Americans like to see how a politician handles the lesser jobs before they trust him with the big one.

Even so, his campaign will be remembered for something positive: he is one more example that no matter how big the bankroll, no one has yet been able to buy the presidency.

Nor will he be forgotten by all the people in all those cottage industries that have grown up around politics.

To them, he will always be one swell customer.

—*February 13, 2000*

## *The Adventures of Bill Clinton*

*To cover the Clinton White House was to cover chaos. It was always something, and when the Monica Lewinsky story broke, it was hard for all of us in Washington to believe. I wrote dozens of commentaries about it, some of which poked fun at the president, others of which came down hard on him. Before Monica, there was Paula Jones. It was in a deposition given in the sexual harassment suit filed by Paula Jones that the president denied an affair with Monica Lewinsky. It was during those days that the White House spin machine opened an attack on Jones. At that point, I had paid little attention to the Jones lawsuit, but when one of the president's allies said, "You never know what you'll find when you drag a hundred dollar bill through a trailer park," I wrote the following essay.*

## MANSION TRASH

As mainstream publications published their advance stories this week about the Paula Jones case, I noticed any number of references to "trailer park trash," "white trailer trash" and quotes about "you never know what you'll find when you drag a hundred dollar bill through a trailer park."

Put aside that Paula Jones didn't live in a trailer, but at a time when we've carried political correctness to nausea-inducing levels, it is a little surprising that we find nothing wrong with stereotyping people by neighborhood. Maybe it should not be surprising because it is just another way to make fun of the poor, the only group in public relations–conscious America that has no spokesman or advocate to fight back.

The Rev. Nathan Baxter, dean of the Washington National Cathedral, noted recently that after the civil rights movement, every sociopolitical movement in America has been by and for the middle- and upper-middle-class professional community. They're good causes all, but in each of them you don't see many poor people involved.

People don't live in trailer parks because they are genetically flawed; it is because they can't afford to live anyplace else. I would also add that I know a lot of nice people who lived in trailer parks and some real trash who lived in big houses.

*—January 12, 1997*

*Nearly two years later I would write the following about Monica Lewinsky.*

## MONICA

Since we spent so much time last week going over the president's words to the grand jury, I decided to spend the weekend going through the e-mail, letters and testimony that Monica Lewinsky gave to the jurors.

I am glad I did. Her tarty public persona aside, what struck me, as she bared her soul to the grand jury, was just how young she was and, for all her fast ways, how vulnerable she seemed. Her worries were the worries of her generation. She worried about her weight, about being taken seriously. And as she wrote to a friend, about finding someone, someday, who would just give her a hug.

Instead, she got tangled up with the president. She became a small part of his life. He became the center of hers. She let herself dream that they might have a future together, lived for the minute or two when he might say something nice to her. When he felt the need and summoned her, she always brought a little gift. One time, she even brought a gift for his dog.

When he gave her little trinkets, she was beside herself. "All my life," she wrote, "everyone has always said I am a difficult person to shop for, yet you manage to choose absolutely perfect presents, gifts for the soul."

All that for a book of poems and some junk, but that's how it is when you're star-struck and hopelessly in love.

I know, I know, what she did was wrong. But I feel sorry for the kid.

—*September 27, 1998*

## *Religion*

*If there is anything more controversial than politics, it is religion, and here are two essays on widely different aspects of religion that drew huge responses from viewers.*

## THE CRISIS IN THE CHURCH

When Cardinal Law stepped down on Friday, the *New York Times* headline said the resignation may well be just the start "as priests and laity challenge the hierarchy."

I hope so. I say that not as a Catholic. I am a Protestant. I do consider myself a religious person, but that too is irrelevant since we do not yet know if God shares that assessment.

So I speak only as an outsider who has spent a lifetime observing politicians and bureaucracies. But I speak as an outsider who loves the Catholic Church for its good works, for being the repository of learning during the Dark Ages and, along with those of the Jewish faith, for shaping the values upon which Western civilization is based.

Believers and nonbelievers alike, we are all the product of those values. The values remain true, and they have stood the test of the centuries. What has gone wrong is what happens so often when bureaucracies become too large and there is no accountability.

Aging leaders have put their own survival ahead of their church's reason for being and in the process forgotten their own history. It was the church bureaucracy's refusal to reform so long ago, after all, that brought about the Protestant movement.

People will seek God in many ways but never in ways that put their children at risk.

Until the church bureaucracy truly comes to terms with that, whatever the cost, and once again places its reason for being ahead of the survival of its leaders, the church as an institution remains at risk.

*—December 16, 2002*

*The following year, I waded into the controversy over the Alabama judge who installed a huge sculpture of the Ten Commandments in the lobby of a courthouse. I expected that many viewers would disagree with my conclusion, but to my surprise, opinion split down the middle, and viewers who agreed with me slightly outnumbered those who did not.*

## THE TEN COMMANDMENTS

As I watched the commotion over the Ten Commandments at the Alabama Supreme Court last week, the thought that kept running through my mind was this: What if Judge Moore had insisted on placing a large statue of the Buddha in the lobby, or perhaps a tribute to Muhammad, the founder of Islam?

That's not so farfetched, you know. There are more Muslims in America than Episcopalians and a sizable Buddhist population.

It is not inconceivable that one day a Muslim will be elected to a U.S. court.

Would Judge Moore's supporters expect a Muslim American judge to keep his religion a personal matter, or would they want him to use it to promote his religion?

I don't question their sincerity or piety, but I hope they have

193

begun to think about that because Islam, like Judaism and Christianity, has been the guiding light now for millions of our citizens.

Someone once said that any religion that needs the help of the state is not a very powerful religion. To suggest that these great religions, which have survived for thousands of years, somehow need or require the state government of Alabama to promote them is not only questionable, it borders on the blasphemous.

The true place of honor for the Ten Commandments is not a state courthouse, but the churches and synagogues of America.

An even better place is deep inside our hearts. To place them otherwise is not to honor but to trivialize them.

*—August 31, 2003*

*Sometimes I write about something or someone simply because they have touched me in some way. That was the reason I wrote one of my earliest commentaries about a young woman I had never met—an angel.*

## THE SHORT LIFE OF ANGEL WALLENDA

It was crowded off the front pages and the newscasts by what may have seemed to be more important news but deep in the pages of the *New York Times* there was a wonderful story about a wonderful life that bears repeating. It was an account of the very short life of Angel Wallenda, who had married into the famous circus family at the age of 17 after surviving a nightmare childhood in which she was beaten and starved and finally overcame drugs.

When her husband-to-be found her scooping ice cream in a shopping mall and invited her to join the family high-wire act, she accepted without hesitation because she said it sounded like a great adventure.

But shortly after she began her training, she developed cancer.

Eventually her right leg was amputated below the knee, and parts of her lung were removed, but she continued training and eventually walked the high wire on an artificial limb. She said she did it "because when I'm way up there in the sky walking on a thin line with a fake leg, people look up at me and really pay attention. They see I'm using everything I've got to live my life the best way I can. It makes them think about themselves and some of them see how much better they could live their own lives.

"Maybe that is my main purpose for being here."

Angel Wallenda was just 28 when the cancer finally got her this week.

Go in any bookstore these days and you'll find shelves filled with books about whether angels really exist.

Well, we know where there is at least one, don't we?

—*May 5, 1995*

## *Holidays*

*I'm still a kid at heart when it comes to holidays. I love Christmas music, the food at Thanksgiving, the fireworks on the Fourth of July and since I have become a grandfather, I must admit that Father's Day has become my favorite.*

## ACTING NORMAL

You can look it up. More telephone calls are made on Mother's Day than any other day of the year. It's a sweet thing to know. Moms deserve it.

But on what day would you guess that most of the collect calls are made? You got it. Father's Day. Paying the bills is just one part of being a dad.

Fatherhood, as every dad knows, is an evolving process. In the early years, we're adored, the ultimate authority on everything. As our children grow older, that changes.

By the teenage years, our children begin to suspect that we don't know anything. It is as if we have become adults without experiencing anything having to do with school, sports, driving, music or certainly the opposite sex.

I'll never forget the first boy-girl party at our house. Mom was complimented on how nice she looked. My instructions were, "Dad, please just act normal."

Has a father, any father, ever told a joke that caused a teenager to laugh? "Dad, at least *try* to act normal!"

So for all the dads, a toast on our day, and there is some good news if you are still in that stage where you're an embarrassment to the entire family. That too passes. Before long, the kids will be telling you again how smart you are, even if they don't believe it, but because they love you. Or maybe they have discovered they have learned a little something from you.

That will make them proud, but by then you'll realize you have learned a lot from them too.

So, Dads, enjoy the day but remember: act normal and don't forget to pick up the check.

—*Father's Day 2002*

*Winston Churchill is one of my heroes, and I love Great Britain and the English people, but I cannot bring myself to take the British royal family seriously—a character flaw, to be sure, but one I proudly share with the founding fathers and one that occasionally crops up in my writing as it did in theirs.*

## WHAT A PRINCE OF A GUY

We have a lot to celebrate on the Fourth of July, but if you needed one more reason, it was right there in the *New York Times*. The *Times* says Prince Charles has been getting so much criticism for being a spoiled eccentric who presides over a corrupt household that for the first time ever, he released a detailed financial statement to show people what they were getting for their money.

Well, the boy has done well! Seventeen million dollars last year from lands and businesses that come with the title, plus another $5 million from the taxpayers, some of which pays the salary of the servant who puts toothpaste on his toothbrush. The statement also lists what the prince does: public appearances, answering letters and such. What it really seems to come down to is that he provides people with an ongoing soap opera, waves and smiles on holidays and if they meet him, the people get a handshake *if* he extends his hand first.

Otherwise don't touch.

So why is this cause to celebrate? Because he's their prince, not ours. It is no news to say that most of the world has come to believe kings and princes are unnecessary, if not downright silly.

But those remarkable people who founded our country figured it out first and changed the world. If they had done nothing else, that was enough.

When I read about Prince Charles, it is always the Fourth of July for me.

—*July 6, 2003*

## *Sports*

*If I have learned one thing since coming to* Face the Nation, *it is that people love their sports. When I did a spoof on the sport of curling, I was overwhelmed by negative e-mail. Don Imus was kidding me about it one morning on his talk show, and I told him I was just glad that people didn't know how little interest I have in basketball. So it was that after the Anaheim Angels eliminated the New York Yankees in the baseball play-offs, I shouldn't have been surprised that my fine piece of poetry was more appreciated on the Left Coast than on the Right One. Even so, I step boldly forward once more to repeat both my poem about the Yankees and my comment on curling.*

## MUDVILLE NORTH

When Mighty Casey swung and missed, indeed, it was a pity,
But it couldn't match the grief that's befallen Gotham City.
Nine to five, that's bankers' hours but also it's the score
That let the Yankees go and rest while others play some more.
Bring out another crying towel, order extra booze.
New Yorkers can't believe it. Their Yankees never lose.
October and no Yankees? Surely, you're delirious.
I think you must be joking. You cannot be world serious.
Ruth is spinning in his grave, Giuliani's in a dither.
And all because Steinbrenner's team for once just ain't a winner.
So now it is to Anaheim that we must tip our topper.
They caused the biggest, richest team to finally come a cropper.
Jeter and Giambi, still fine lads, strong and true,
But in the new world Left Coast rules. Whatever can we do?
Yep, there is no joy in Mudville, but Yanks to ease the pain
Remember it's not winning that always leads to fame.
Remember Mighty Casey who fanned the air that day.
Not really what he wanted, if he had had his way.
But had old Casey not struck out and gone on to lose the game
I doubt that any of the rest of us would even know his name.

—*October 6, 2002*

*One e-mailer on the West Coast was upset because I referred to it as the Left Coast, which he said showed that I was trying to picture Los Angeles as "Communist." It was my friend, the novelist Dan Jenkins, who taught me the term Left Coast, a phrase he based on standing in our mutual home town, Fort Worth, Texas, and looking north. "Los Angeles is on your left, and New York is on the right," he told me. "What else would you call it?"*

## OLYMPIC CURLING

I know everyone else is worried about skating, but here is my Olympic question: What is all this about curling? As I went to bed the other night, they were curling. I got up at 5:30 and there was more curling or maybe it was a tape of the same curling.

And what is curling, anyway? My wife wandered by the television the other night and said, "Are they bowling on ice?" No, and they are not waxing the floor with those long-handled squeegees. Nor are they skating without skates.

They are sliding around on the ice in their shoes the way we used to do it as kids when we would slide down the hall in our socks.

They tell me curling is very big in Canada, but what this looks like to me is something that people do so they can have a beer afterward. Whatever it is, it is beyond me. The teams strategize, and they slide those little smudge pots or tea kettles or whatever they are down the ice and then the announcer says, "It's four to nothing." But I have no idea why. The other night the announcer described a lady curler as the Roger Clemens of curling. Said she liked to throw the high, hard one. Say what? Roger Clemens? I know it's my fault, but I am missing something here.

Maybe the Summer Olympics will be more my thing. I hear they're thinking about miniature golf.

*—February 17, 2002*

*More and more I find myself starting sentences with the phrase, "Maybe I'm just getting older but I've come to believe . . ." and in fact, I am getting older, and it has changed my way of thinking about many things. That's probably good news, but as any person who is getting on will tell you, the aging process is not all good news. Still, it does have its advantages, which caused me to offer the following.*

# ON THE ADVANTAGES OF GROWING OLDER
## (AND THERE AREN'T MANY,
## SO WRITE THESE DOWN)

I am in the stage of life where I spend most of my time trying to keep the list of things I can do longer than the list of things I can't, and let me tell you, it requires a lot more maintenance than it used to: walking on a treadmill, taking my various pills and reading all those nutrition facts printed in that tiny type on packaged food, which got me to wondering, Is there anything positive about becoming more mature, as it were? And in fact, I have decided there is.

Growing older reduces the number of things we have to worry about—for example, which brand of motorcycle is most likely to be stolen. I heard on the radio there is a new study about that, but I no longer need to know the answer.

Nor do I need to know how old Britney Spears really is or whether she's had some work done. I no longer need to worry about whether tattoos are safe or the best place to get body parts pierced or where to find low-rider blue jeans or whatever happened to Monica Lewinsky or whether Bill Clinton wore boxers, briefs or jammies with feet on them.

No, moving toward the sunset of life brings a certain clarity, a winnowing out of what's important and what isn't. Probably the most important thing is realizing we no longer have to worry about being cool.

Of course, we do have to worry about our families having us frozen.

*—August 1, 2002*

*The one real advantage to growing older is the memories. This commentary is about one of my favorites.*

## LIGHTS OUT

One rainy night last week, we were visiting friends, and after dinner the lights went out. We figured it was just the weather and they'd come back on soon, so we just kept talking in the dark and listening to the rain.

The lights never came back, but here's the surprising part: it didn't ruin the evening; it made it better. It reminded all of us of when we were children. Before television, before air conditioning, when families went to the front porch after dinner to cool off. We all remembered sitting in the dark for hours, talking, looking at the stars, hearing things the grown-ups didn't know we heard because they thought we had nodded off.

Today, we live in the information age, but we're so bombarded with so much information from all sides now—from the television, the radio, the Internet—it all becomes a distraction. Sitting in the dark the other night, it was as if we were freed from all that.

The conversation got better because our imaginations came into play, and we could pause from time to time just to listen to the rain.

I must also confess the discovery of another secret delight: when it's dark, you can close your eyes at any point in the conversation without offending anyone.

Very relaxing.

*—June 24, 2001*

*Some of the commentaries that have had nothing to do with the headlines of the moment have often drawn the greatest response. I put them in the "have you noticed" category—the essays about those little shifts in our culture that we sometimes fail to see in the beginning but come to take for granted—cell phones being example number one. I began to realize the enormous changes that cell phones were having on our culture while in a New York restaurant several years ago. Three people were talking on cell phones at one table. I wondered if they were talking to each other ("How's the swordfish?" Or maybe, "Pass the salt"). Later, in the men's room, I heard the beep, beep, beep of someone making a call from one of the stalls. I didn't want to think about how that call began. ("Honey, I was just sitting here thinking about you . . ." or perhaps, "No, that isn't a broken water main you hear in the background. It's well . . . it's . . .")*

*Whatever the case, here is my take on cell phones.*

## THE NEW CIGARETTES

First, a disclosure: I have a cell phone, and it is a great way to stay in touch. But two weeks on the road has convinced me that staying in touch is not why people have cell phones. No, cell phones are the new cigarettes, the crutch we lean on when we're nervous. Something to fiddle with when we have nothing to do with our hands. Think about it. Back when we all smoked, the first thing we did when we got off an airplane was grab a cigarette.

Now we grab a cell phone.

The hold these things have on us is stronger than nicotine. The other day, I watched a man try to take off his coat on a moving train and put it in the overhead rack while talking on his cell phone.

Did you ever try to take off your coat one-handed?

Many cell phone calls come down to no more than this: "Here is where I am at this very minute, and I'll call you later," which is harmless enough. But here is why I worry: Sooner or later someone will decide these things are bad for you, because that is what someone always decides, and they will be banned, which means the sidewalks of New York—a city of tall buildings surrounded by young women smoking cigarettes—will be jammed up even more by people coming outside to use their cell phones.

This will leave the rest of us no choice but to walk in the streets where we'll have to dodge all those drivers using their cell phones.

This is not good.

—*October 2003*

15

———

# They Made It Happen

## The Correspondents and Producers
### of *Face the Nation*

*Around the world thoughts shall fly in the twinkling of an eye.*

Anonymous

*The Correspondents*

There have been eight moderators of *Face the Nation*, seven men and one woman, since that first broadcast on November 7, 1954. All of us were veteran correspondents when we came to *Face the Nation*. Each of us shared a love for the news, but no two of us were alike.

How different were we? Let me tell you a story about Martin Agronsky, who anchored the broadcast in the mid-1960s.

Most professional broadcasters develop a keen sense of time. Told to say something in 45 seconds, we learn to say whatever needs to be said within a second or two of that. It becomes second nature to us. Somehow we know how many seconds have passed without looking at a clock. Walter Cronkite was the best I ever knew at it. The world could be collapsing around him, but if a producer told him to "give me 30 seconds" Walter could ad-lib and hit the mark exactly, time after time.

*Ted Koop, 11/7/54–8/14/55.*

*Stuart Novins, 8/21/55–11/6/60.*

Agronsky was a globe-trotting, broadcasting legend and also a true eccentric who sometimes seemed to be in a different world. For sure, he missed class the day they taught broadcasters about time. He had no sense of how long it takes to say anything.

During his time as moderator of *Face the Nation*, he also anchored several of the Sunday hourly newscasts on radio. The problem was that the newscasts would end, and Agronsky would still be reading. Engineers finally hit on a plan to correct the problem. Ten seconds before the newscast ended, the engineer would hold up a sign that said, "This is Martin Agronsky, CBS News in Washington."

Agronsky would see the sign, pause, and sign off the broadcast with those words.

One Easter Sunday, the engineer on duty decided to give the sign a seasonal touch and changed it to, "This is Peter Rabbit, CBS News in Washington."

Agronsky saw the sign and ended the newscast, with those exact words.

There are no tapes of that newscast, but the story was told to me as true. (It is such a good story that I never checked it further.) Whatever the case, every moderator put a personal stamp on the broadcast, and in most cases, the style reflected the journalism of the time.

Ted Koop, the CBS News Washington Bureau chief, the first

moderator, could not have been more different from the spacey Agronsky. Koop was a convivial insider's insider and president of the National Press Club. Washington journalism was a clubby, all-male bastion in those days and Koop's popularity with his fellow journalists and easy familiarity with government officials exemplified that.

George Herman, who headed the broadcast from 1969 to 1983, longer than any other moderator, had been too young for World War II when "Murrow's boys" made their marks. But when he was sent off to cover the Korean War, he became a model for the dashing philosopher-correspondents who had come to symbolize CBS News.

When I came to the Washington Bureau in 1969, Herman was known as the office encyclopedia. He seemed to know something about everything, and during his long run on *Face the Nation*, he covered foreign royalty and every important figure in American politics. Because he was so serious, I was stunned when I asked him one day what his favorite broadcast had been.

*Howard K. Smith, 11/14/60–4/20/61.*

"You're going to be surprised," he told me, "but it was the interview with Muhammad Ali."

Ali was at the height of his powers and popularity. As the poetry-reciting heavyweight champion of the world, he was also big news, and *Face the Nation* considered it something of a coup to land him for an interview.

Even so, Herman said, no one

*Paul Niven, 11/17/63–4/11/65.*

205

*Martin Agronsky, 7/11/65–12/29/68.*

*George Herman, 2/02/69–9/11/83.*

knew what to expect when Ali arrived with dozens of body-guards, hangers-on and advisers. And he was huge.

"He was so beautifully pro-portioned, I had no idea how big he was," Herman said. "But he was big—he looked seven feet tall and when he went into our little makeup room to get some pow-der on his nose, he took up the whole room, literally."

When one of Ali's advisers tried to come in the room with him, there was no room for makeup artist Marge Hubbard.

"He could not have been more gentle," Hubbard said, "but he was a gentle giant, and it was all kind of intimidating."

Herman got worried during the microphone checks before the program went on the air. As Herman told it:

"He looked gloomy and glow-ering and was shaking his head and I said, 'What's the problem Mr. Ali?' and he said, 'Oh god, I shouldn't have agreed to this, you guys are gonna murder me.' In one of my brighter moments, I said, 'Mr. Ali, if I could put on the gloves and got into the ring with you, would you murder me?' and he said, 'Oh no, we'd have a little fun and I'd show you some things and we'd have a good time.' So I said, 'Mr. Ali, what makes you think I'm a bigger son of a bitch than you are?' And he brightened up and smiled, and we did the show."

It was perhaps the first and only time that a guest's preshow jitters had been calmed by assurances that the moderator was no more a son of a bitch than he was.

In 1997 I had my first and only interview with a boxer—heavyweight champion Riddick Bowe, who had announced earlier that week that he intended to join the Marine Corps and go to boot camp to show his patriotism. Unlike Ali's entertaining interview with Herman, Bowe's appearance was more or less a disaster, which, to her credit, producer Carin Pratt had predicted it would be. I thought it would be interesting to know why a celebrity who had won millions of dollars in the boxing ring wanted to become a private in the Marine Corps. Bowe was friendly enough, but his diction was so poor it was all but impossible to understand anything he said. Nor did he seem to know exactly why he wanted to join up. Nonetheless, he did enlist the next week. His Marine career did not last long. He flunked basic training and was released after eleven days. Later, he was arrested for kidnapping his wife and transporting her across state lines during a domestic dispute. That led to an eighteen-month federal prison sentence.

*Lesley Stahl, 9/18/83–4/14/91.*

Lesley Stahl, the moderator from 1983 to 1991, was the first —and to date the only—woman to serve in that position. Her interviewing technique was in sharp contrast to Herman's cerebral style. Where Herman sometimes saw a duty to calm guests,

*Bob Schieffer, 4/26/91–present.*

207

Stahl welcomed controversy. When *TV Guide* called her Sunday morning's toughest interviewer, she was delighted.

Ted Koop, the first moderator, had not intended to stay long in the job. As Washington news director for CBS, he already had plenty to occupy him as one of the company's key executives, and in September 1955, he hired Stuart Novins to replace him on *Face the Nation*. Novins anchored the broadcast until November 6, 1960, when—in that cruel way that seems to be a mark of television—he read in the newspaper that the program was being overhauled and that Howard K. Smith would be replacing him as moderator.

To his dismay, Novins learned the story was true. He had a long, distinguished career at CBS, including the exclusive interviews with Khrushchev and Castro, and despite his abrupt removal from *Face the Nation*, he went on to other prestigious assignments. When he retired in 1975 after 35 years, he had been the recipient of more than 50 awards for public affairs reporting.

Novins's replacement, Howard K. Smith, had been one of Murrow's boys who covered World War II. Smith's tenure on *Face the Nation* was a short one. He headed the broadcast from November 14, 1960, until April 20, 1961, a period in which the broadcast underwent its most radical changes. Under a new format, Smith moderated a weekly debate on various issues—such as the role of government and whether Communist China should be admitted to the United Nations. The program was expanded to an hour but removed from its Sunday time slot and rescheduled in prime time. Competing against entertainment programs, it quickly sank in the ratings and was canceled in five months.

When *Face the Nation* returned to its familiar Sunday time slot on November 11, 1963, a CBS News veteran named Paul Niven was named moderator and anchored the broadcast until September 11, 1965. Five years later, he died at age 45 when fire swept his Georgetown home.

Niven was succeeded by Agronsky, who presided over the broadcast from July 11, 1965, to December 29, 1968. When he died in 1999, the *Washington Post* called him "one of the best . . . at talking head programs." He was also one of the most traveled. He worked at NBC, ABC and CBS and when he left CBS began a syndicated program, *Agronsky and Company*, the first of the programs to feature a group of correspondents who interviewed each other rather than newsmakers.

Agronsky was succeeded by George Herman, who in turn was succeeded by Lesley Stahl. In April 1991, I was named to replace Stahl when she was named a coeditor on *60 Minutes*.

## The Producers

Carin Pratt, the current longtime producer of *Face the Nation*, will never forget the first time she met face to face with Betty Phelan, press secretary to Louisiana Senator John Breaux.

"I thought your name was Prattagin," the astonished Phelan said.

The two women quickly figured out how the mix-up had occurred.

Several weeks earlier, Pratt had been trying to track down Phelan to book Breaux for a *Face the Nation* interview. Phelan had been out of pocket and returned to her office to find 10 voice mails from Pratt, each of which began, "It's Carin Pratt again."

"I thought that was her name," Phelan said, "Pratt-again."

Just call her Pratt, please. But no other story better illustrates what *Face the Nation* producers do or the determination and doggedness they bring to the job. Once we finish a broadcast on Sunday morning, Carin, senior producer Denise Li and I begin thinking about who we should interview for next Sunday's broadcast. What is the big story likely to be? Who is available and willing to talk about it? By Monday morning, the third member of the team, producer Arlene Weisskopf, begins making the preliminary calls. By Wednesday, we hope to have a fix on what the broadcast will be about. By Friday, Carin will have left dozens of "it's Pratt again" messages.

Through the years, the moderators have put the face on *Face the Nation*, but the producers who work behind the scenes are the unsung heroes and heroines who week after week, year after year, track down that hard-to-find guest, book the satellites, order the limos to pick up the guests and get the broadcast on the air.

*The current* Face the Nation *team. (l-r) senior producer Denise Li, associate producer Kelly Rockwell, executive producer Carin Pratt, director Clyde Miles, producer Arlene Weisskopf. (Karin Cooper–Polaris Images for CBS)*

The year 2004 marks Pratt's twentieth on *Face the Nation*, the longest tenure of anyone who has ever been part of the broadcast. She joined *Face the Nation* as an assistant producer after a stint as a copyeditor at the *Washington Post*. She became executive producer in 1993. A mother of two teenage boys, she somehow finds the time to run *Face the Nation* and still attend all the baseball, soccer and squash games in which her boys play. Her number two at *Face the Nation*, senior producer Denise Li, came to the broadcast three years after Pratt and does much of the research for each show. Weisskopf came to the broadcast in 1993. Like Carin and Denise, she spends most of her day on the phone, keeping tabs on the availability and whereabouts of the people who make the news. The fourth member of our team is associate producer Kelly Rockwell, who supervises the *Face the Nation* flashback features we began in 2004. She also did much of the research for this book, including the compiling of a list of every person who has appeared on *Face the Nation.*

Being a *Face the Nation* producer has not been a job for the timid, the faint of heart or those who are willing to take no for an answer.

Ted Ayers was the first producer and perhaps the only one who was held at gunpoint while the broadcast was in progress. That happened during the exclusive interview with Fidel Castro, as reported in Chapter 3. Ayers also played a major role in landing the exclusive interview with Khrushchev.

Michael J. Marlow succeeded Ayers. He had produced various public affairs programs for CBS. It was in 1961 that Fred Friendly was given responsibility for the program and converted it into a weekly debate. I have not listed Friendly as one of the producers of the broadcast since he was there only a few months and only when the program's longtime interview format had been junked.

*Ted Ayers, the broadcast's first producer, briefs young Harvard professor Henry Kissinger for Kissinger's first appearance on the broadcast in 1957.*

Producer Prentiss Childs's long association with *Face the Nation* began in 1963. The son of Marquis Childs, the syndicated Washington columnist for the *St. Louis Post-Dispatch*, Childs had been the producer of *Lamp unto My Feet*, an award-winning CBS religious broadcast, before coming to *Face the Nation*. He had also produced numerous specials embracing ballet and drama. It was hardly the kind of thing to prepare him for the hair-raising adventures he experienced during his 11 years at *Face the Nation*.

The bomb set off outside his hotel room in Saigon, recounted in Chapter 6, was only one of his narrow escapes. He and reporter Martin Agronsky were later caught in the cross-fire of a gunfight in the Dominican Republic, and in 1967, he flew to Athens to interview

*One of producer Mary Yates's Middle East contacts helped her snare a rare interview with Yasir Arafat.*

Greek publisher Helen Vlachos, who had been critical of the military government. Childs learned on arrival that the government had placed her under house arrest and refused to allow her to be interviewed. The government offered its own spokesman instead, and Childs had no choice but to interview him. That led to one of the weirdest demands ever. Afteward, the government did not like what its own spokesman had said and demanded "equal time" to rebut him. By then, Childs was safely back in the United States, and the demand was denied.

*Joan Shorenstein Barone, who produced* Face the Nation *during the early 1980s, knew more about politics than anyone who was ever associated with the broadcast. She died of cancer at age 38. (Shorenstein family photo)*

During the first five years he served as executive producer of the broadcast, Childs was assisted by Ellen Wadley, a 15-year veteran of the CBS News Washington Bureau, who served as coproducer.

In 1967, Sylvia Westerman, a veteran of the Washington Bureau with wide contacts throughout the government, replaced Wadley as coproducer and remained with the broadcast until May 12, 1974, when she and Childs both left the network. Westerman later became a vice president of NBC News under Bill Small, who had been CBS Washington Bureau chief before going to NBC.

*Face the Nation* has always been broadcast live when the broadcast originated in Washington, and every live broadcast carries a risk. Anything can go wrong and sometimes does, but Mary O. Yates, who succeeded Childs, was known for never leaving anything to chance.

She was the widow of NBC producer and documentary maker Ted Yates, who had been killed while covering the Six-Day War in

Jerusalem. She became producer of the broadcast on September 22, 1974.

On the Sunday that Muhammad Ali was the guest, Yates feared he might cancel at the last minute, and she convinced Minnesota senator Walter Mondale to stand by and be prepared to go on if Ali didn't show.

It takes a certain clout to convince a U.S. senator to play second fiddle to anyone, but Yates pulled it off.

Joan Shorenstein, an incurable confessed political junkie and CBS news researcher, replaced Yates and produced the broadcast during the last years of Herman's tenure, and she supervised the transition when Lesley Stahl replaced Herman as moderator in 1983.

Shorenstein was a tireless worker, and her encyclopedic knowledge of politics was exceeded only by that of her husband, Michael Barone. Barone is the author of *The Almanac of American Politics*, an annual publication that has become the definitive work on the demographics and political history of all 435 congressional districts. *Face the Nation* never had a better fix on politics than when Shorenstein produced it. Tragically, she succumbed to cancer at the age of 38. After her death, her family established the Shorenstein Center on the Press, Politics and Public Policy at the Kennedy School of Government at Harvard in her memory.

After Shorenstein's death, Karen Sughrue, one of the original producers at CNN when it went on the air in 1980, joined the broadcast. CBS News executives decided she was too young, however, to be called the executive producer, so that title was given to Jonathan Ward, a news executive in New York. After several years of seasoning, she was given the title. She and Lesley Stahl traveled the world interviewing officials ranging from Yasir Arafat to Boy George. Stahl once said Sughrue had two great advantages: "She was patient and she was tall." Sughrue's deputy during most of this period was Jeanne Edmunds, who also had wide contacts in Washington. Shortly before I came to the broadcast in 1991, Marianna Spicer-Brooks, who had been a producer on David Brinkley's rival broadcast at ABC, replaced Sughrue. She helped me get comfortable in the moderator's chair, and when she departed on December 12, 1993, she was replaced by Pratt.

That *Face the Nation* has survived for half a century is testament to the skill and dedication of each person who has been a part of the broadcast.

CHAPTER 1: IN THE BEGINNING

The bulk of this chapter comes from personal interviews conducted over the past three years with Frank Stanton (with whom I spoke three times), Don Hewitt, Andy Rooney, Daniel Schorr, George Herman and Walter Cronkite. To round out my impressions of the Paley and Stanton relationship, I also drew on Corydon B. Dunham's book, *Fighting for the First Amendment: Stanton of CBS vs. Congress and the Nixon White House* (Praeger, 1997), as well as Sally Bedell Smith's *In All His Glory: The Life of William S. Paley* (Simon & Schuster, 1990).

I also drew on the resources of the CBS News Library, which has an extensive collection of newspaper clippings about *Face the Nation* that have been assembled over the years. My thanks to librarian Carol Parnes for her help in guiding me to the right ones. For all of the transcripts that were faxed and mailed, thanks to Cryder Bankes and Joan Fitzsimons. Thanks also to CBS News director of audience services Ray Faiola and members of his staff who contributed: Nancy Delaney, Marion Philpot and especially John Behrens. They maintain a file of *Face the Nation* press releases going back to the first broadcast, which proved to be a treasure trove of information. Sandy Genelius of the CBS News Press Office and her deputy, Andie Silvers, compiled a chronology of major events in the history of the network, which also proved invaluable. My thanks to them for many hours they spent tracking down details and photos that made this a better book. This project would not have been possible without the help of Nancy Eichenbaum and David Lombard of the CBS Photography Archives. Statistics cited in this chapter and throughout the rest of the book (the total number of broadcasts, and the list of all the guests who have appeared) are the result of long hours of work by Kelly Rockwell, who did most of the basic research for this book. She did it the old-fashioned way: she started with the first broadcast and simply wrote down the name of each guest and how many times he or she had appeared. She said it is an assignment she will remember for the rest of her life. Knowing how many long days she devoted to it, she earned both my sympathy and my sincere thanks.

CHAPTER 2: IN THE AGE OF FEAR

The account of McCarthy bringing a pistol to a *Meet the Press* interview comes from *Meet the Press* by Rick Ball (McGraw-Hill, 1998). For this chapter, I also drew on Fred Friendly's book, *Due to Circumstances Beyond Our Control* (Random House, 1967). A lengthy interview with Andy Rooney and a letter he wrote me describing the atmosphere of those times were especially helpful. Newspaper and trade publication reviews of the first broadcast are on file in the CBS Library. A. M. Sperber's *Murrow: His Life and Times* (Freundlich Books, 1986) and Alexander Kendrick's *Prime Time: The Life of Edward R. Murrow* (Little, Brown, 1969) remain the definitive works on Murrow, and I referred to them many times as I wrote this book.

CHAPTER 3: THE BIG SCOOP

Details on how the interview was arranged came primarily from the interview with Dan Schorr and CBS News press releases published at the time. Schorr also wrote about the interview in his books *Staying Tuned* (Pocket Books, 2001) and *Clearing the Air* (Houghton Mifflin, 1977). The study commissioned by the Fund for the Republic on the impact of the interview is on file at the CBS News Library. Reactions to the broadcast from public officials are taken from the report. An audio recording of Stanton's speech to the National Press Club can be found at the Library of Congress.

CHAPTER 4: THE MEN OF LOVE PUT ON A REALLY BIG SHOW
The story of Sullivan's relationship to Murrow and his desire to be a part of the CBS News team was completely unknown to me when I began this book. I stumbled onto it one day while going through news clips in the CBS News Library. I found a clip from the now-defunct *New York Journal-American* that had appeared the day after the *Face the Nation* and Sullivan interviews were broadcast. A columnist noted it had been "Castro day at CBS." I wondered what that meant and contacted *CBS Sunday Morning* contributor John Leonard, who had written a book about Sullivan, *A Really Big Show* (Viking Press, 1992). He remembered Sullivan had interviewed Castro and had mentioned it in his book but said a book by Sullivan's longtime producer, Marlo Lewis, might have more details. With the help of CBS librarian Carol Parnes, I found Lewis's out-of-print book, *Prime Time* (Tarcher, 1979). Lewis laid out the story in some detail, and it was my main source for what became my favorite story in the book. The direct quotes come from Lewis's book. I found more detail about it in another book about Sullivan, *A Thousand Sundays* (Putnam, 1980), by Jerry Bowles. His book was the main source for how Sullivan stood down the Soviet bureaucracy in Moscow. An audio version of Sullivan's interview can be found on several web sites. My thanks to Andrew Solt and his staff—Belinda White, Greg Vines, Gary Salem and Beatrice McMillan—at Andrew Solt Productions and SOFA Entertainment, which controls the rights to Sullivan's work for permission to use the photo of Sullivan with Castro. The account of Che Guevara's visit to *Face the Nation* comes from an interview with Prentiss Childs, the broadcast's long-time producer.

CHAPTER 5: COVERAGE A LONG TIME COMING
Most of this chapter is based on the transcripts of the broadcasts of that era. Interviews with Childs and longtime CBS News Capitol

Hill correspondent Roger Mudd helped me to understand the politics of the time. Howard K. Smith's troubles with the CBS brass are well documented in Fred Friendly's book *Due to Circumstances Beyond Our Control*, and other books about CBS.

## Chapter 6: Vietnam

As with the previous chapter, the bulk of the research on this one came primarily from reading the transcripts of the broadcasts. For me, the greatest surprise was to discover how many times the officials who came on *Face the Nation* to talk about Vietnam either did not know what they were talking about or simply misled viewers about what was happening. It was also interesting to me to discover that Secretary of Defense Robert McNamara never appeared on the broadcast.

## Chapter 7: For Want of a Question

Melvin Laird was again generous with his time as he was during the writing of my memoir, *This Just In: What I Couldn't Tell You on TV*. One of these days I'll remember to ask him every question that should be asked about that day on *Face the Nation* when I should have brought up the Pentagon Papers. Ben Bradlee, the former *Washington Post* editor, and Neil Sheehan, who wrote the *New York Times* summaries of the Pentagon Papers, also gave me invaluable help. I had previously heard most of the Nixon White House tapes of the phone calls on the Sunday the papers were published, but they have been assembled in logical order on the web site of an organization called the National Security Archive. I found their work very helpful and referred to it often in writing this chapter.

## Chapter 8: Badgering George Shultz

This chapter is the direct result of a happy accident and dogged research. I had completely forgotten about Lesley Stahl's interview with Shultz and ran across it one day while searching the transcripts for information on another subject. I found it so compelling that I decided it deserved a chapter of its own to illustrate not only how a government official's appearance on *Face the Nation* had changed policy but as an example of the changing role of women in journalism and politics. Independently, executive producer Carin Pratt had found the interview of Senator Margaret Chase Smith and suggested it would make a fine ending for the chapter. She was right. George Herman told me of the encounter with Golda Meir. As noted in the chapter, I also drew on Stahl's memoir, *Reporting Live* (Simon & Schuster, 1999), and Shultz's book, *Turmoil and Triumph: My Years as Secretary of State* (Scribner, 1993), as well as a conversation with my friend Lesley.

CHAPTER 9: THE SUNDAY PRIMARIES
Herman told me of the episodes involving Eagleton and Scranton when they appeared on *Face the Nation*. I also exchanged correspondence earlier with Eagleton about his Sunday interview when I was writing my memoir. Theodore White wrote about Eagleton's appearance on *Face the Nation* in the 1972 edition of his *Making of the President* series (Atheneum, 1973). He wrote about Scranton's travails in his 1964 edition. Churchill's quip about fireside chats comes from William Manchester's book, *The Last Lion* (Little, Brown, 1988). I have covered every presidential campaign since 1972 and also relied on my memory of those times.

CHAPTER 10: THE LONGEST STORY AND CHAPTER ELEVEN:
AT WAR AT HOME AND ABROAD
During that period I was covering Capitol Hill and Congress for the CBS Evening News, so much in these chapters comes from my own memory and experiences. I was the lead reporter covering the impeachment proceedings for CBS. Among other things, I had the dubious honor of reading much of the Starr Report aloud on television the day it was released publicly.

CHAPTER 12: THE WAR IN IRAQ
For this chapter, I drew on interviews with Andrew Heyward, the president of CBS News; Marcy McGinnis, senior vice president;

Washington, D.C., vice president and bureau chief Janet Leissner; correspondents John Roberts, Scott Pelley and Thalia Assuras, and cameraman Don Lee; and *60 Minutes II* producer Bill Owens. A conversation with Secretary of Defense Donald Rumsfeld helped me to understand how the embed program was conceived. The quotations from Ed Murrow came from NPR correspondent Bob Edwards's new book, *Edward R. Murrow and the Birth of Broadcast Journalism* (Wiley, 2004).

### CHAPTER 14: MY THOUGHTS EXACTLY
The commentaries come from my own musings, but as I wrote at the beginning of the chapter, my wife, Pat, often comes up with ideas that spark my imagination, just one of the many things that she has done over the 37 years of our marriage to make my life so great.

### CHAPTER 15: THEY MADE IT HAPPEN
This chapter comes from CBS biographies of those involved and personal interviews with Ellen Wadley, George Herman, Prentiss Childs, Lesley Stahl, Jeanne Edmunds and Carin Pratt. One of the most pleasant parts of researching this book came in reconnecting with Childs and Herman, neither of whom I had seen in years.

### The DVD
I am glad we included the DVD. *Face the Nation*, after all, is a television program, and TV programs are better watched than read, an assertion I feel qualified to make after reading hundreds of the broadcast transcripts. Even when it's a broadcast you love, reading TV program transcripts is a tedious undertaking I would wish on no one. I am grateful to CBS vice president Linda Mason for her guidance on the project. I asked CBS News Washington Bureau chief Janet Leissner to produce the DVD. She graciously agreed and did her usual outstanding job. Among her many other contributions to the book, Kelly Rockwell coordinated the project. Special thanks also to Siobhan Lockhart, who tracked down many of the tapes, and to Roy Carubia and his staff in CBS Archives who located many oth-

ers and formatted them for broadcast use. Thanks also to my friend Charlie Wilson, as fine a videotape editor as I have ever worked with. He gave the DVD his special touch and many of the still photos in the book were captured from videotape by Charlie. He was assisted in assembling the final product by Joni Mazer-Field, another outstanding editor.

Finally, I thank Super Agent Esther Newberg for her superb work on my behalf, and Rob Weisbach of Simon & Schuster. He is a fine editor, and his suggestions made this a better book and DVD.

## GUESTS APPEARING OVER LONGEST
## TIME SPAN ON *FACE THE NATION*

| Guest | Span in Years |
|---|---|
| Henry Kissinger | 43 |
| Edward Kennedy | 35 |
| Donald Rumsfeld | 34 |
| Abba Eban | 31 |
| Ralph Nader | 30 |
| King Hussein I of Jordan | 29 |
| Robert J. Dole | 29 |
| Barry Goldwater | 28 |
| Daniel P. Moynihan | 28 |
| Dick Cheney | 27 |
| Hamilton Jordan | 25 |
| Howard Baker | 25 |

*Young Senator Ted Kennedy, 1968.*

*Senator Ted Kennedy on a recent* Face the Nation *broadcast.*

| Guest | Span in Years |
|---|---|
| James Baker | 24 |
| Sam Nunn | 22 |
| Jacob Javits | 22 |
| Mike Mansfield | 22 |
| Alexander Haig | 21 |
| Lloyd Bentsen | 20 |
| J. William Fulbright | 19 |
| John McCain | 18 |
| Andrew Young | 17 |
| Zbigniew Brzezinski | 16 |
| John Tower | 16 |

*Secretary of Defense Donald Rumsfeld checking the time.*

## GUESTS MAKING THE MOST APPEARANCES
## ON *FACE THE NATION*

| *Guest* | *# of Appearances* |
| --- | --- |
| Robert J. Dole | 62 |
| John McCain | 51 |
| Leon Panetta | 39 |
| Orrin G. Hatch | 35 |
| Joseph R. Biden | 35 |
| Patrick Buchanan | 28 |
| Joseph I. Lieberman | 27 |
| Trent Lott | 27 |
| Christopher J. Dodd | 26 |
| Richard G. Lugar | 26 |
| Henry M. Jackson | 25 |
| James Baker | 23 |
| Hubert H. Humphrey III | 22 |

*Ralph Nader in a 1970 appearance.*

*Bob Dole's first appearance, in 1971.*

| Guest | # of Appearances |
|---|:---:|
| Phil Gramm | 22 |
| Tom Daschle | 22 |
| Arlen Specter | 22 |
| Dick Gephardt | 22 |
| Patrick J. Leahy | 21 |
| Dick Cheney | 21 |
| William J. Bennett | 21 |
| Howard Baker | 20 |
| Al Gore, Jr. | 20 |
| George Mitchell | 19 |
| Newt Gingrich | 18 |
| Reverend Jesse L. Jackson | 18 |

*Senator Howard Baker, former Senate Majority Leader, and later Ronald Reagan's chief of staff, took his own photos when he came on the show in 1980.*

*Dick Cheney has appeared on* Face the Nation *while serving as assistant to the president, representative from Wyoming, secretary of defense, and vice president.*

## ABOUT THE AUTHOR

BOB SCHIEFFER is chief Washington correspondent for CBS News and anchor and moderator of *Face the Nation*. He has won six Emmy awards, and in 2002, he was named Broadcaster of the Year by the National Press Foundation and elected to the Broadcasting Hall of Fame. The *New York Times* bestselling author of *This Just In* and *The Acting President* (with Gary Paul Gates), Schieffer lives in Washington, D.C.

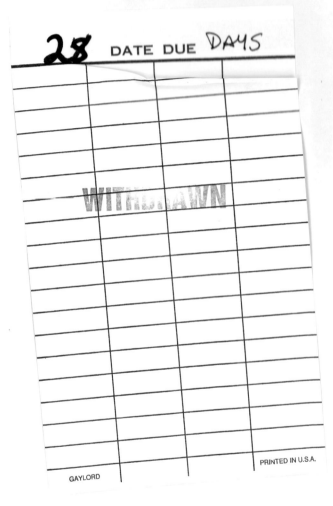

**28** DATE DUE *DAYS*

GAYLORD

PRINTED IN U.S.A.